Shakespeare's
MACBETH

by
DAVID SHELLEY BERKELEY
PROFESSOR OF ENGLISH
OKLAHOMA STATE UNIVERSITY
Author of *Blood Will Tell in Shakespeare's Plays*
and other works on Milton and Shakespeare

with Summaries of Plot and Characterization
by
Arthur Gewirtz
Leonora Brodwin

Simon & Schuster, Inc.
15 Columbus Circle
New York, NY 10023

DISTRIBUTED BY PRENTICE HALL TRADE SALES

Manufactured in the United States of America

1 2 3 4 5 6 7 8 9 10

ISBN 0-671-68761-1

Monarch and colophon are trademarks
of Simon & Schuster, Inc.

CONTENTS

THE LIFE OF WILLIAM SHAKESPEARE

Facts versus speculation. Anyone who wishes to know where documented truth ends and where speculation begins in Shakespearean scholarship and criticism first needs to know the facts of Shakespeare's life. A medley of life records suggest, by their lack of inwardness, how little is known of Shakespeare's ideology, his beliefs and opinions.

William Shakespeare was baptized on April 26, 1564, as "Gulielmus filius Johannes Shakspere"; the evidence is the parish register of Holy Trinity Church, Stratford, England.

Husband and father. On November 28, 1582, the Bishop of Worcester issued a license to William Shakespeare and "Anne Hathwey of Stratford" to solemnize a marriage upon one asking of the banns providing that there were no legal impediments. Three askings of the banns were (and are) usual in the Church of England.

On May 26, 1583, the records of the parish church in Stratford note the baptism of Susanna, daughter to William Shakespeare. The inference is clear, then, that Anne Hathaway Shakespeare was with child at the time of her wedding.

On February 2, 1585, the records of the parish church in Stratford note the baptisms of "Hamnet & Judeth, sonne and daughter to William Shakspere."

Shakespeare insulted. On September 20, 1592, Robert Greene's *A Groats-worth of witte, bought with a million of Repentance* was entered in the Stationers' Register. In this work Shakespeare was publicly insulted as "an upstart Crow, beautified with our ["gentlemen" playwrights usually identified as Marlowe, Nashe, and Lodge] feathers, that with *Tygers hart wrapt in a Players hyde* [a parody of a Shakespearean line in *II Henry VI*] supposes he is as well able to bombast out a blank verse as the best of you: and beeing an absolute *Iohannes fac totum*, is in his owne conceit the onely Shake-scene in a countrey." This statement asperses not only Shakespeare's art but intimates his base, *i.e.*, non-gentle, birth. A "John factotum" is a servant or a man of all work.

On April 18, 1593, Shakespeare's long erotic poem *Venus and Adonis* was entered for publication. It was printed under the author's name and was dedicated to the nineteen-year-old Henry Wriothesley, Earl of Southampton.

On May 9, 1594, another long erotic poem, *The Rape of Lucrece*, was entered for publication. It also was printed under Shakespeare's name and was dedicated to the Earl of Southampton.

On December 26 and 27, 1594, payment was made to Shakespeare and others for performances at court by the Lord Chamberlain's servants.

For August 11, 1596, the parish register of Holy Trinity Church records the burial of "Hamnet filius William Shakspere."

From "villein" to "gentleman." On October 20, 1596, John Shakespeare, the poet's father, was made a "gentleman" by being granted the privilege of bearing a coat of arms. Thus, William Shakespeare on this day also became a "gentleman." Shakespeare's mother, Mary Arden Shakespeare, was "gentle" by birth. The poet was a product of a cross-class marriage. Both the father and the son were technically "villeins" or "villains" until this day.

On May 24, 1597, William Shakespeare purchased New Place, a large house in the center of Stratford.

Cited as "best." In 1598 Francis Meres's *Palladis Tamia* listed Shakespeare more frequently than any other English author. Shakespeare was cited as one of eight by whom "the English tongue is mightily enriched, and gorgeouslie invested in rare ornaments and resplendent abiliments"; as one of six who had raised *monumentum aere perennius* [a monument more lasting than brass]; as one of five who excelled in lyric poetry; as one of thirteen "best for Tragedie," and as one of seventeen who were "best for Comedy."

On September 20, 1598, Shakespeare is said on the authority of Ben Jonson (in his collection of plays, 1616) to have been an actor in Jonson's *Every Man in His Humour*.

On September 8, 1601, the parish register of Holy Trinity in Stratford records the burial of "Mr. Johannes Shakspeare," the poet's father.

Becomes a "king's man." In 1603 Shakespeare was named among others, the Lord Chamberlain's players, as licensed by James I (Queen Elizabeth having died) to become the King's Men.

In 1603 a garbled and pirated *Hamlet* (now known as Q1) was printed with Shakespeare's name on the title page.

In March 1604, King James gave Shakespeare, as one of the Grooms of the Chamber (by virtue of being one of the King's Men), four yards of red cloth for a livery, this being in connection with a royal progress through the City of London.

In 1604 (probably) there appeared a second version of *Hamlet* (now known as Q2), enlarged and corrected, with Shakespeare's name on the title page.

On June 5, 1607, the parish register at Stratford records the marriage of "M. John Hall gentleman & Susanna Shaxspere," the poet's elder daughter. John Hall was a doctor of medicine.

Becomes a grandfather. On February 21, 1608, the parish register at Holy Trinity, Stratford, records the baptism of Elizabeth Hall, Shakespeare's first grandchild.

On September 9, 1608, the parish register at Holy Trinity, Stratford, records the burial of Mary Shakespeare, the poet's mother.

On May 20, 1609, "Shakes-peares Sonnets. Never before Imprinted" was entered for publication.

On February 10, 1616, the marriage of Judith, Shakespeare's younger daughter, is recorded in the parish register of Holy Trinity, Stratford.

On March 25, 1616, Shakespeare made his will. It is extant.

On April 23, 1616, Shakespeare died. The monument in the Stratford church is authority for the date.

Buried in Stratford church. On April 25, 1616, Shakespeare was buried in Holy Trinity Church, Stratford. Evidence of this date is found in the church register. A stone laid over his grave bears the inscription:

> Good Frend for Iesus Sake Forbeare,
> To Digg The Dust Encloased Heare!
> Blest Be Y^e Man Y^T Spares Thes Stones,
> And Curst Be He Y^T Moves My Bones.

Demand for more information. These are the life records of Shakespeare. Biographers, intent on book length or even short accounts of the life of the poet, of necessity flesh out these (and other) not very revealing notices from 1564–1616, Shakespeare's life span, with ancillary matter such as the status of Elizabethan actors, details of the Elizabethan theaters, and life under Elizabeth I and James I. Information about Shakespeare's artistic life—for example, his alteration of his sources—is much more abundant than truthful insights into his personal life, including his beliefs. There is, of course, great demand for colorful stories about Shakespeare, and there is intense pressure on biographers to depict the poet as a paragon of wisdom.

Anecdotes—true or untrue? Biographers of Shakespeare may include stories about Shakespeare that have been circulating since at least the seventeenth century; no one knows whether or not these stories are true. One declares that Shakespeare was an apprentice to a butcher, that he ran away from his master, and was received by actors in London. Another story holds that Shakespeare was, in his youth, a schoolmaster somewhere in the country. Another story has Shakespeare fleeing from his native town to escape the clutches of Sir Thomas Lucy who had often had him whipped and sometimes imprisoned for poaching deer. Yet another story represents the youthful Shakespeare as holding horses and taking care of them while their owners attended the theater. And there are other stories.

Scholarly and certainly lay expectations oblige Shakespearean biographers often to resort to speculation. This may be very well if biographers use such words as *conjecture*, *presumably*, *seems*, and *almost certainly*. I quote an example of this kind of hedged thought and language from Hazelton Spencer's *The Art and Life of William Shakespeare* (1940): "Of politics Shakespeare seems to have steered clear . . . but at least by implication Shakespeare reportedly endorses the strong-monarchy policy of the Tudors and Stuarts." Or one may say, as I do in my book *Blood Will Tell in Shakespeare's Plays* (1984): "Shakespeare particularly faults his numerous villeins for lacking the classical virtue of courage (they are cowards) and for deficiencies in reasoning ability (they are 'fools'), and in speech (they commit malapropisms), for lack of charity, for ambition, for unsightly faces and poor physiques, for their smell, and for their harboring lice." This remark is not necessarily biographical or reflective of Shakespeare's personal beliefs; it refers to Shakespeare's art in that it makes general assertions about the base—those who lacked coats of arms—as they appear in the poet's thirty-seven plays. The remark's truth or lack of truth may be tested by examination of Shakespeare's writings.

Who wrote Shakespeare's plays? The less reputable biographers of Shakespeare, including some of weighty names, state assumptions as if they were facts concerning the poet's beliefs. Perhaps the most egregious are those who cannot conceive that the Shakespearean plays were written by a person not a graduate of Oxford or Cambridge and destitute of the insights permitted by foreign travel and by life at court. Those of this persuasion insist that the seventeenth Earl of Oxford, Edward de Vere (whose descendant Charles Vere recently spoke up for the Earl's authorship of the Shakespearean plays), *or* Sir Francis Bacon, *or* someone else wrote the Shakespearean plays. It is also argued that the stigma of publication would besmirch the honor of an Elizabethan gentleman who published under his own name (unless he could pretend to correct a pirated printing of his writings).

Ben Jonson knew him well. Suffice it here to say that the thought of anyone writing the plays and giving them to the world in the name of Shakespeare would have astonished Ben Jonson, a friend of the poet, who literally praised Shakespeare to the skies for his comedies and tragedies in the fine poem "To the Memory of My Beloved Master the Author, Mr. William Shakespeare, and What He Hath Left Us" (printed in the First Folio, 1623). Much more commonplace and therefore much more obtrusive upon the minds of Shakespeare students are those many scholars who are capable of writing, for example, that Shakespeare put more of himself into Hamlet than any of his other characters or that the poet had no rigid system of religion or morality. Even George Lyman Kittredge, the greatest American Shakespearean, wrote, "Hamlet's advice to the players has always been understood—and rightly—to embody Shakespeare's own views on the art of acting."

In point of fact, we know nothing of Shakespeare's beliefs or opinions except such obvious inferences as that he must have thought New Place, Stratford, worth buying because he bought it. Even Homer, a very self-effacing poet, differs in this matter from Shakespeare. Twice in the *Iliad* he speaks in his own voice (distinguished from the dialogue of his characters) about certain evil deeds of Achilles. Shakespeare left no letters, no diary, and no prefaces (not counting conventionally obsequious dedications); no Elizabethan Boswell tagged Shakespeare around London and the provinces to record his conversation and thus to reveal his mind. In his plays Shakespeare employed no *raisonneur*, or authorial mouthpiece, as some other dramatists have done: contrary to many scholarly assertions, it cannot be proved that Prospero, in *The Tempest* in the speech ending "I'll drown my book" (Act V), and Ulysses, in *Troilus and Cressida* in the long speech on "degree" (Act II), speak Shakespeare's own sentiments. *All characters in all Shakespearean plays speak for themselves. Whether they speak also for Shakespeare cannot be proved because documents outside the plays cannot be produced.*

As for the sonnets, they have long been the happy hunting ground of biographical crackpots who lack outside documents, who do not recognize that Shakespeare may have been using a persona, and who seem not to know that in Shakespeare's time good sonnets were supposed to read like confessions.

Some critics even go to the length of professing to *hear* Shakespeare speaking in the speech of a character and uttering his private beliefs. An example may be found in A. L. Rowse's *What Shakespeare Read and Thought* (1981): "Nor is it so difficult to know what Shakespeare thought or felt. A writer, Logan Pearsall Smith, had the perception to see that a personal tone of voice enters when Shakespeare is telling you what he thinks, sometimes almost a raised voice; it is more obvious again when he urges the same point over and over."

But there's no proof! Rowse, deeply enamoured of his ability to hear Shakespeare's own thoughts in the speeches of characters speaking in character, published a volume entitled *Shakespeare's Self-Portrait, Passages from His Work* (1984). One critic might hear Shakespeare voicing his own thoughts in a speech in *Hamlet*; another might hear the author in *Macbeth*. Shakespearean writings can become a vast whispering gallery where Shakespeare himself is heard *hic et ubique* (here and everywhere), without an atom of documentary proof.

"Better So." Closer to truth is Matthew Arnold's poem on Shakespeare:

> Others abide our question. Thou art free.
> We ask and ask—thou smilest and art still,
> Out-topping knowledge. For the loftiest hill,
> Who to the stars uncrowns his majesty,
> Planting his steadfast footsteps in the sea,
> Making the heaven of heavens his dwelling
> Spares but the cloudy border of his base
> To the foiled searching of mortality;
> And thou, who didst the stars and sunbeams
> know,
> Self-schooled, self-scanned, self-honoured, self-
> secure,
> Didst tread the earth unguessed at.—Better so. . . .

Here Arnold has *Dichtung und Wahrheit*—both poetry and truth—with at least two abatements: he exaggerates Shakespeare's wisdom—the poet, after all, is not God; and Arnold fails to acknowledge that Shakespeare's genius was variously recognized in his own time. Jonson, for example, recorded that the "players [actors of the poet's time] have often mentioned it as an honor to Shakespeare, that in his writing (whatsoever he penned) he never blotted a line" (*Timber*), and of course there is praise of Shakespeare, some of it quoted above, in Meres's *Palladis Tamia* (1598).

The best approach. Hippocrates' first apothegm states, "Art is long, but life is short." Even Solomon complained of too many books. One must be, certainly in our time, very selective. Shakespeare's *ipsissima verba* (his very words) should of course be studied, and some of them memorized. Then, if one has time, the golden insights of criticism from the eighteenth century to the present should be perused. (The problem is to find them all in one book!) And the vast repetitiousness, the jejune stating of the obvious, and the rampant subjectivity of much Shakespearean criticism should be shunned.

Then, if time serves, the primary sources of Shakespeare's era should be studied because the plays were not impervious to colorings imparted by the historical matrix. Finally, if the exigencies of life permit, *biographers of Shakespeare who distinguish between fact and guesswork*, such as Marchette Chute (*Shakespeare of London*), should be consulted. The happiest situation, pointed to by Jesus in Milton's *Paradise Regained*, is to bring judgment informed by knowledge to whatever one reads.

INTRODUCTION TO
MACBETH

Theme. There are few plays from which all critics will abstract the same main theme. With this caveat one may think that *Macbeth* is founded on *the idea that the nature of man and the nature of man's universe are so constructed that a man cannot play with evil and remain prosperous and intact in this world*, not to mention the next one. More precisely, in the words and formulation of G. R. Elliott, it is that a "wicked intention must in the end produce wicked action unless it is not merely revoked by the protagonist's better feelings, but entirely eradicated by his inmost will, aided by Divine grace." *The theme is enforced* by the brevity of the play; by the relatively unvaried style; by recurrent images, notably sleeplessness, blood, and darkness; and by a succession of physically thrilling actions, such as sleepwalking, hallucinations, Banquo's ghost, the Sisters, deaths and reports of deaths.

Dating of Macbeth. The dating of *Macbeth* is not definitely established. The intimate connections of the play with the ideas of James I of England suggest that the play was not written before 1603, the date of James's accession. One Simon Forman attended a performance at the Globe in 1611. *Tres Quasi Sibyllae*, in which creatures like the Sisters spoke oracularly of James's splendid descent from Banquo, was given before the King in the summer of 1605. The Porter refers to "equivocation," thought to allude to Father Garnet's "equivocation" during his trial in the spring of 1606 for complicity in the Gunpowder Plot; and this note of equivocation, since it resounds throughout the play, does not appear to be a spur-of-the-minute insertion. A connection may exist between the farmer that hanged himself on the expectation of plenty (II.iii.4–5) and the price of wheat in 1606. The evidence therefore intimates that *Macbeth* was first produced in late 1606.

Sources of **Macbeth.** The main source of *Macbeth* is Raphael Holinshed's *Chronicles*, 1587 from which, as a modern source (as distinguished from Plutarch the ancient, for example), Shakespeare felt free to depart. He combines the rebellion of Macdonwald and the invasion of Sweno, King of Norway. He drops Holinshed's point that Banquo was Macbeth's chief ally in the murder of Duncan. He shifts over to the murder of King Duff by Donwald for the account of the butchery of Duncan. He seems to take the voice crying "Sleep no more" from what Holinshed tells of the dream of King Kenneth III. In Holinshed, the Weird Sisters disappear after meeting Macbeth on the heath. Wizards in Holinshed warn to beware Macduff, and a witch offers the prophecy of "none of woman born" and the prophecy of Birnam Wood. Shakespeare eliminates Holinshed's point that Macbeth was a good king for ten years.

Other chroniclers presenting the story of Macbeth were Hector Boece, *Scotorum Historiae*, 1527, translated into Scottish by John Bellenden; John Fordun, *Scotichronicon*, ca. 1384; and Andrew Wyntown, *Orygynale Chronykil of Scotland*, ca. 1424. Although the history of Macbeth was known, there does not seem to have been an earlier play on this subject. As one might expect, Shakespeare employed many minor sources or, at any rate, wrote in such fashion that scholars frequently suggest analogues that they are tempted to view as sources. For example, Jane H. Jack calls attention to the Book of Revelation (on a portion of which King James wrote his *A Fruitfull Meditation*) as paralleling, in its account of Satan's breaking forth from prison and the terrors of the last days, Macbeth's reign in Scotland. She goes on to suggest that both works are full of images of the withdrawal of grace, vast space, strange phenomena (voices, earthquakes, etc.), blood, and children. Henry N. Paul, perhaps the most notable recent scholar of *Macbeth*, suggests Senecan influence specifically from *Hercules Furens*, in the horror of Macbeth and Lady Macbeth as they look upon their bloodstained hands. He thinks Seneca's words "Curae leves loquuntur, ingentes stupent" (light cares make one talkative, huge cares stupefy) underlie Malcolm's lines in IV.iii.209–210. More generally, Paul connects the ghosts, the aphorisms, and the tendency to make the audience admire Macbeth at the last hour with the practice of Seneca.

An actor's play. Macbeth is preeminently an actors' play because its condensed expression leaves much to pauses, hesitations, inflections, and gestures, especially in III.iv. Dennis Bartholomeusz' *Macbeth and the Players* may be offered in testimony. Garrick played the title role so as to inspire fear and pity. Kemble emphasized pity by the nobility of his acting. Macready's Macbeth was more savage than noble. G. H. Lewes wrote of Kean's Macbeth: "You had less the thought of a combat with Fate than of a bull fight and of the brave and frantic efforts of the tortured animal in the arena." Orson Welles in a filmed version made Macbeth a heathen of the moors more suitable to the atmosphere of *Beowulf* than to the Renaissance. Roman Polanski in another filming made Macbeth so villainous that the protagonist does not struggle between the promptings of good and evil. In Akira Kurosawa's filmed version, Lady Macbeth announces pregnancy when Macbeth is about to become king.

Questions that the play raises. Macbeth, like other good tragedies, raises many questions for which there are no completely satisfactory answers. Why does Macbeth not know of Cawdor's treachery? Why does Macduff leave his family? Who is the Third Murderer? Why does Banquo never speak to the lords of the prophecies of the Sisters? Why does Banquo, the putative ancestor of King James, show a less healthy moral sensibility than Macduff, particularly inasmuch as he has more evidence of Macbeth's guilt than Macduff possesses? Does Macbeth's attitude toward his wife change as the play proceeds? Has Lady Macbeth had a child? How is one to reconcile the beneficent and the malefic aspects of external nature in *Macbeth*? What has Hecate to do with manifestations of witchcraft in Scotland? Is *Macbeth* to be thought as having medieval Scotland or the Renaissance as its chronological setting? How can Duncan be thought a highly admirable king when he does not always know his friends from his enemies? How do we know that a Jacobean audience understood that the posterity of Banquo and of Duncan somehow merged, inasmuch as this notion is extra-textual? Why does Lady Macbeth, who shows little interest in Macbeth's account of the Witches, suddenly invite demons to possess her? Did Shakespeare know that the word "weird" signified fate? How long does the action of *Macbeth* last? Why is there evidence of at least six unwritten scenes in *Macbeth*? Why does Macbeth speak of himself in IV.i.98 as "our high-placed Macbeth" when it is not characteristic of him to refer to himself impersonally? How could the Bleeding Sergeant travel the impossibly long way from Fife to Forres (I.ii.42)? Precisely what is the action indicated by the stage directions at the end of V.viii?

Witchcraft on the English stage. Before *Macbeth* only a few English plays, such as *Mother Bombie* and *The Wise Woman of Hogsden*, had dealt at length with witchcraft, and the only great play to be devoted to the supernatural during the English Renaissance before Shakespeare's work was Marlowe's *The Tragical History of Doctor Faustus*. Nevertheless, assuming *Macbeth* to have been tailored to King James's interests and believing that English people of these times generally credited witchcraft, we think that Shakespeare had a number of considerations that made success possible for a play combining witchcraft and the supernatural. James was a student of witchcraft, as attested by his writing *Daemonologie*, published in 1597. In 1605 the King visited Oxford University where he witnessed a playlet in Latin in which three persons dressed as sibyls came forth to flatter him with prophecies concerning the tenure of the Stuart dynasty. The primary source of *Macbeth*, Holinshed, authorized use of the three Sisters in a dramatic treatment of this subject. Holinshed says: "But afterwards the common opinion was, that these women were either the weird sisters, that is (as ye would say) the goddesses of destinie, or else some nymphs or feiries, indued with knowledge or prophesie by their necromanticall science, bicause every thing came to passe as they had spoken." Shakespeare causes the Sisters to absorb later prophecies vouchsafed Macbeth by a wizard and a witch, thus magnifying their role.

How old is Macbeth? Macbeth's age has often been mooted by scholars, and the question obtrudes itself upon readers and, all the more so, upon film directors and directors of plays. A too-young Macbeth and Lady Macbeth, as in Roman Polanski's filmed version, may be "too callow to express Shakespeare's emotions" (Pauline Kael, *New Yorker*, Feb. 2, 1972); and Macbeth thus depicted may be at his latter end too unwrinkled and supple to be natural in delivering such lines as "my way of life/Is fall'n into the sear, the yellow leaf. . . ." A too-old Macbeth and Lady Macbeth, as in George Schaefer's filmed version (with Maurice Evans and Dame Judith Anderson), seem past the age of political ambition. In discussing this question in an appendix to *Shakespearean Tragedy*, A. C. Bradley concluded that Macbeth is middle-aged, older than Malcolm, of about the same age as Banquo, and younger than Duncan.

Macbeth's character. Macbeth has, as his wife says, the milk of human kindness (which was not a cliché when the play was written), the kind of affection that many people have for others when self-interest is not rampant. He has a high regard for Duncan and Banquo, defaming the latter only once (III.i.74 ff.). He differs from Duncan in this regard in that the King's charity is of a quality that works to transform human society into a family and that, as G. R. Elliott points out, "makes the spirit of Duncan persist through the play after his death." Nevertheless, Macbeth shares in a somewhat limited way in the moral nature of manhood as seen in I.vii.46–47, as E. M. Waith observes, without wanting to contract himself at the urgings of his wife into a paragon of energy, energy simply devoted to utterly selfish ends. Macbeth thus differs from Macduff, who more fully realizes both the valorous and moral nature of manhood, and from Richard III, who is a melodramatic villain and indeed a scourge of God.

Macbeth, unlike Richard, is not completely hardened even at the end of the play. He exhibits remorse immediately after the murder of Duncan, and he repeatedly displays anguish after commission of his atrocities. In proposing the savage murder of Macduff's family, he speaks of these "unfortunate" souls (IV.i.152) without attaching irony or sadism to this adjective. The passage "I have lived long enough" (V.iii.22–28) is not, in its apprehension of the failure of a life, the utterance of a thorough reprobate like Richard; and "poor heart" (V.iii.28) is analogous to "unfortunate souls." Macbeth, unlike Richard, is self-tortured and thus wins of us a degree of sympathy. Macbeth is utterly free from Richard's savage humor as seen, for example, in his jesting about sending Clarence to Heaven post-post-haste. Unlike Iago, Macbeth is unequipped with a philosophy of egoism.

Unlike Lady Macbeth, he does not pray to have his nature altered. He makes no formal compact, as Faustus does, with the Devil. He never chastises his wife for her failure to bear sons though his ambition is dynastic rather than personal, and even though, whatever Renaissance medical theory may have taught, royal practice as observable in the reign of Henry VIII held the wife rather than the husband to blame for lack of issue. Although there is slight evidence that Macbeth uses Lady Macbeth not to form his murderous intent toward Duncan but to give him courage and practical insight into the way this piece of regicide may be committed, he vacillates before the murder of Duncan (I.vii.1 ff.), he experiences hallucinations that precede (II.i.33–35) and follow (II.ii.35–36) this murder; he is unable to answer "amen" to "God bless us" (II.ii.23 ff.); he feels remorse in II.ii.60 ff.; and his later savagery suggests the utter subversion of his nature.

Macbeth is not sufficiently cultivated in good or evil to muster poise for all occasions: thus he experiences difficulty in sleeping; he uses rhetoric badly in the presence of others when disturbed (I.iv) and even resorts to improbability (*e.g.*, I.iii.149–150); he cannot reproduce imperial dignity and the graces of kingship as Claudius, Hamlet's stepfather, manages to do. So he must act, and so he stays the onset of madness, acquiring firmness of purpose in the wrong road. Even his soliloquies, notable for magniloquence and phantasmagoria and marked by voluptuous word-painting, show more the stages of his corruption than its causes—the need for action to cover his lack of poise in awaiting developments and the need to stifle the moral imagination that enables him to foresee the consequences of his actions.

Audience sympathy for Macbeth. Shakespeare manages to keep Macbeth within the circle of the readers' sympathy in spite of the difficulties inherent in blackening his character (as received from Holinshed, the primary source) in the interest of promoting the Stuart myth and of thereby caressing and cosseting King James. Shakespeare suppresses the point that it is an elected king, Duncan, who names his son heir-apparent. He declines to mention Holinshed's remark about Duncan's "feeble and slouthful administration." We hear nothing of Macbeth's capable rule of Scotland for ten years as reported by Holinshed. Shakespeare causes Macbeth to murder a guest, whom he is duty-bound to protect. He makes a younger and physically stronger man murder a presumably old man in his sleep. He causes Macbeth to murder, only for the cause of advancement, a king who is legitimate and honorable, and this murder is compassed on the night of the day when Macbeth has been rewarded with the thanedom of Cawdor and his wife has been given a diamond by the monarch. Macbeth is insensitive to the beauty of nature and, with qualifications, to the beauty of human life. His imagination fixes on the horrid and gloomy.

In spite of these refractory considerations, *Shakespeare wins by various means a measure of sympathy for Macbeth.* He gives his protagonist wonderful lines. He exhibits Macbeth's virtue and bravery at the beginning of the play, and he keeps Macbeth's bravery before us to his death. He emphasizes the influence of the supernatural on Macbeth. He makes much of the inordinate ambition of Lady Macbeth and of her goading Macbeth by remarks that reflect badly on his manhood. Shakespeare reduces our interest in most other characters by keeping them relatively unindividualized so that Macbeth and Lady Macbeth tend to absorb our attention and sympathy. *He keeps Macbeth and Lady Macbeth active: audiences tend to identify themselves more readily with active than with passive characters.* He keeps the murder of Duncan offstage. He keeps Macbeth from becoming a scourge of God like Richard III: if Macbeth is a monster of iniquity from the beginning, as in Orson Welles's *Macbeth*, the speech about the loss of friends, honour, love (V.iii.24–26), and certain other speeches become drained of significance. Readers of Romantic ideology and sympathies, because of their sympathy with anyone who is a rebel and who dares greatly, tend to feel kindly toward Macbeth. Critics whose forte is character analysis, *e.g.*, Bradley, incline to admire Macbeth. On the other hand, those who are chiefly concerned with pattern analysis, notably of imagery (Christian references, light, darkness, order, disorder, etc.), are not especially sympathetic with Macbeth. (See also "Macbeth" in "Character Analyses," p. 136.)

Character of Lady Macbeth. Lady Macbeth derives from her counterpart in Holinshed, more from Donwald's wife (Donwald was "set on" by his wife to murder King Duff) in the same source, possibly from Livy's Tullia, and mostly from Shakespeare. Extremes of her characterization are on the one side a hatchet-faced termagant and on the other, as G. H. Lewes said of Mrs. Siddons' post-Shakespearean sentimentalization, "a fair, delicate *womanly* woman, capable of great 'valour of the tongue', capable of nerving herself for any one great object but showing by her subsequent remorse and broken heart that she had been playing a part." The former characterization has explicit textual basis in Malcolm's "fiend-like queen" (V.ix.35); the latter is based upon the belief that she is small—she says that she has a small hand—and probably fragile, that she is beautiful, and that she almost faints after the murder.

Lady Macbeth is of course not so thoroughly individualized as Macbeth: accordingly Shakespeare does not show her gradual declension. She defines herself wholly by her husband, whom she will single-mindedly promote by any means to the throne, in which he seems to have shown a tenacious interest before the opening of the play in speeches not reported in the exposition. If she does not have considerable force of character, compounded of "self-conquest, singleness of will, and tenacity of purpose," she will appear sniveling, and Macbeth will not seem misled. She is neither intellectually brilliant nor very knowledgeable. Her idea of blaming the grooms lacks cogency. Like people of humdrum minds, she depends on proverbial wisdom, *e.g.*, "the poor cat i' the adage." The Witches are not important to her although they are made important in the play. Interestingly, Lady Macbeth and the Witches are visually linked in Kurosawa's filmed version by "unearthly whiteness both in dress and countenance." She does suffer a traditional effect of demon-possession in that by removal of her blood she is unable to have children—*in Shakespeare villains do not usually beget offspring*—in spite of her husband's intense desire to found a dynasty, and loss of blood may account for her tottering of mind and body in her last appearance. Shakespeare, with his habitual aversion to the excessively repulsive, does not explain concerning either Lady Macbeth or Joan of Arc how demons remove blood from human females.

Lady Macbeth is like Lady Macduff in remoteness from the political life of Scotland, in her passionate and impatient nature, and in her devotion to her husband; she lacks, of course, Lady Macduff's conventional morality but not to the point of speaking of Duncan's murder without the disguise of euphemisms (*e.g.*, "to catch the nearest way," "this night's great business"). Though her nature is sufficiently poised to indulge deliberate punning ("I'll gild the faces of the grooms withal"), she is not able to endure horrors which are unplanned and novel, *e.g.*, the butchery of Duncan's grooms. She eggs on her husband by charm, coaxing, soothing, and taunting. An interesting point is what she means by *sworn* in "had I so sworn as you / Have done in this" (I.vii.58–59). Either she means that Macbeth has actually sworn before the opening of the play to kill Duncan because "he would not have been chosen by the witches had his soul not been prepared for them," or Lady Macbeth is exaggerating in the hope of steeling her husband for the deed.

The three sisters. The precise nature of the Sisters is ultimately unclear, an enrichment of the play because a great tragedy should by no means be so clear to us as the multiplication tables lest it cease to fascinate us and lest it oversimplify human nature, to say nothing of the supernatural. Holinshed spoke of the Sisters as "feiries," and Shakespeare paralleled "fairies" and "tempters of the night" in *Cymbeline*, II.ii.9, thus employing in *Macbeth* traditional associations of these creatures and eschewing the delicate, dainty, and entrancing ambience of fairies that he had innovated in *A Midsummer Night's Dream*. The term *weird* (from Anglo-Saxon *wyrd*, "fate") in "weird sisters," twice spelled *weyward* in the First Folio of 1623, means in Holinshed "goddesses of destinie," but this fact does not necessarily mean that Shakespeare gives the word Holinshed's meaning. Certainly the idea that the Sisters are Fates lends them stature far above that of witches as understood by the English and assists in deluding Macbeth to his downfall. When his destruction is near he realizes that they are "juggling fiends," creatures through whom the Devil works. It was one of the errors of the great Shakespearean scholar G. L. Kittredge, who, interestingly, wrote *Witchcraft in Old and New England* (1929), to insist upon the Nornlike (*i.e.*, resembling the Norse Fates) character of the sisters (*Sixteen Plays of Shakespeare* [Boston, 1946), pp. 589–60): the fact is that *they do not determine Macbeth's destiny but only predict it.*

Yet, unlike witches, they can disappear into exiguous air; and they seem to know the past, the present, and the future. Yet they are like *English witches (who are properly to be distinguished from Scottish witches*) in their horrid appearance and in the disgusting ingredients thrown into their brew. Among themselves they speak as if they came from the lowest classes, but with Macbeth they speak in elevated fashion with obscure brevity and solemnity in headless octosyllabics. Their oracular utterance presumably derives from the inspiration of their "familiars" (one of whom is named "Harpier"). The puzzling identity of the Sisters is compounded by the Hecate scenes, which are usually thought to be non-Shakespearean interpolations by Thomas Middleton because of his authorship in *The Witch* of the songs called for in the stage directions at III.v.33 and IV.i.43; but it is by no means certain that Middleton wrote the nonlyrical portions of these scenes.

Macbeth *and the Bible.* Shakespeare wrote for an audience that was steeped in the Bible and for a king who was not only later to be the dedicatee of the Authorized Version (in the United States called the King James Version) but also at the time of the play, a profound Biblical scholar. *Macbeth*, though not so overtly theological as Marlowe's *The Tragical History of Doctor Faustus*, is the *Shakespearean tragedy most saturated in Biblical reference.*

As Paul N. Siegel has observed, *Macbeth resembles Adam* in being suggested to evil by demonic forces, in the deliberate choice of evil which seems good, in his desire to rise in the scale of being, and in susceptibility to wifely logic. Thus his characterization is universalized and made applicable to everyman. Evil in Macbeth is given the same wide reference by the protagonist's linkage with Judas, Lucifer, and Saul. *Macbeth is like Judas* in that his victim, Duncan, is a Christ-figure overflowing with love and grace; in his welcome at Dunsinane to Duncan as being reminiscent of Judas at the Last Supper; and in the earthquake and eclipse that accompany the crucifixion of Christ and the murder of Duncan. *Macbeth is like Lucifer (Satan)* in that both fall because of ambition to be kings; in their dismay at hearing that someone else (the preincarnate Christ in the history of Lucifer, and Malcolm in *Macbeth*) is designated for kingly promótion; and in their brightness before falling in their respective realms into outer darkness; note too Malcolm's speaking of himself as "a weak, poor, innocent lamb" (IV.iii.16). Analogs *connecting Macbeth to Saul* are the murderous and moody nature of the two men, their consultation of witches who raise spirits for them, their falling in battle, and their decapitation. Jane H. Jack suggests that Shakespeare tells the story of Macbeth not so much in terms of violation of the political chain of being as in those involving in destruction a king who has allied himself (like his archetype Saul) to the delusive powers of evil rather than the true God.

Appeal of the play. The appeal of *Macbeth* derives from many considerations. It is a short play, having been custom-made for King James, who favored short plays; and it is perhaps true for people in general, as it was for the ancient Greeks, that a long book is a great evil. The play, like Greek tragedy, has a short (and at times ambiguous) exposition although Shakespeare could hardly assume that his English audience knew as much of Macbeth's story as Greek tragedies presumed of the knowledge of the myths upon which they were almost exclusively based. Shakespeare, in other words, appeals to that numerous group of spectators and readers who speedily tire of what they regard as fatiguing preparations and who desire very soon to be confronted with the main conflict of the play. Accordingly the play is notably economical, and partly because of this it gains and keeps a high degree of intensity. The language is most felicitous—almost everywhere one looks, but especially in the speeches of Macbeth, the phrasings are so memorable that the text is almost a collection of purple patches; yet the language conduces to characterization and thematic statement rather than existing for itself.

Macbeth himself fascinates people because he is a type not in the sense of the miserly old man, the braggart soldier, and the cunning servant of Roman comedy but because he belongs to an organization—the Scottish political establishment—and therefore has a "boss," whom he considers murdering and whom he does murder. Much of mankind has bosses, and perhaps every-one at some time idly wonders what would happen to him if the boss were removed by murder or otherwise.

SCENE-BY-SCENE CRITICAL
ANALYSIS OF *MACBETH*

Introductory note on references. In Shakespearean criticism,
an *act* is identified by a Roman capital numeral: for example, I.
A *scene* is identified by a Roman lowercase numeral: *e.g.*, iii.
Lines are identified with Arabic numbers: *e.g.*, 10–25. Thus,
I.iii.10–25 means Act I, Scene iii, lines 10–25.

When lines are discussed with act and scene understood, the
word *line* is abbreviated "l." and *lines* "ll:" *e.g.*, l. 10, ll. 10–25.

The line numbers used in the following discussion may vary
somewhat from those used in some school editions.

Names of critics mentioned in this discussion are usually
connected with their writings listed in the Annotated Bibliogra-
phy, page 162.

ACT I, SCENE i

Plot summary. The play opens with a meeting of Three Witches
in some sort of deserted place. The Witches tell us that the next
time they meet it will be with Macbeth. The meeting will take
place when the tumult ("hurlyburly") is ended, when a battle has
been "lost and won," and that this will occur before the sun goes
down. After having said this, the Witches hear the cries of their
"familiar spirits," two of whom are called Graymalkin and
Paddock, recite an ambiguous couplet ("Fair is foul and foul is
fair: / Hover through the fog and filthy air"), and exeunt.

Critical analysis. Shakespearean scenes at their beginnings plunge into the midst of things, leaving the reader to gather what has immediately preceded; the opening of *Macbeth* is an instance. The Witches have had a consultation and are about to depart. The question of the First Witch about whether to meet "In thunder, lightning, or in rain"(l. 2) suggests that these witches by their spells cause bad weather, an idea confirmed in I.iii.20–25 and IV.i.52–60. One may say that *Macbeth* gains in dramatic force if *the reader or spectator makes the imaginative effort of taking the Witches seriously.* The "battle" that the Second Witch refers to is that taking place this day between the forces of Duncan, King of Scotland, and those of Macdonwald, the Hebridean rebel, and Sweno of Norway. The battle is lost from the Witches' point of view when Macdonwald is slain by Macbeth, and it is won when Sweno is driven from Scotland: it is not difficult to understand why the Witches would sympathize with rebellion, but why the Witches are opposed to Sweno's invasion of Scotland—the point is H. N. Paul's—is unclear. "The battle's . . . won" would not allude to the death of Duncan or the flight of his sons because these are events of the night.

Macbeth here presents the "weird sisters" in the character of the three Fates, but the play does not always sustain this conception of their role. As M. C. Bradbrook points out, *Macbeth*'s witches derive from many different traditions: the "weird sisters" of Holinshed; the North Berwick coven of witches (in their control of weather, sailing in a sieve); the magician's power to command spirits and foretell the future; English witches (beards, animal familiars, petty revenge against the sailor and his wife); the ability to vanish like bubbles (herein they differ from common witches); and freedom from subjection to superior demons (though spirits raised in the cauldron are called "our masters" [IV.i.63]).

Whether the Witches are human or not is unclear. The Third Witch mentions meeting Macbeth, establishing the supernatural control of the play, especially the force of metaphysical evil upon Macbeth in *this first of English plays to treat witchcraft seriously*. Then the First Witch, hearing a cat, says, "I come, Graymalkin," naming her familiar spirit, *i.e.*, demonic servitor. The Second Witch hears her familiar spirit, whom she names "Paddock," presumably the "hedge-pig" or hedgehog of IV.i.2. Because toads cry out under torture may be (in part) why G. L. Kittredge and G. B. Evans think Paddock to be a toad when the Second Witch says, "Paddock calls." The Third Witch's familiar is named "Harpier," as we learn from IV.i.3, presumably from harpy. Harpier's shape is not indicated here or elsewhere, but it is probably that of an owl since this bird hooted during the night of Duncan's murder. The Third Witch hears his distinctive note just before l. 10 and answers "Anon." There is no stage direction to indicate that the audience hears anything, but a producer of *Macbeth* may call for the sound of an owl.

Moral relativity. "Fair is foul, and foul is Fair" (l. 11) introduces the idea of moral relativity, of deceptiveness of appearances, and, as L. Veszy-Wagner says, of Macbeth's "uncertain identity" *e.g.*, whether to be loyal or disloyal to the King, whether he is a manly or an effeminate man). Here *Shakespeare's master-theme for all his dramatic work*—the deceptiveness of appearances—is in view. In Roman Polanski's filmed version of *Macbeth*, one of the Three Witches is "fair" and youthful, her two companions being traditionally "foul." One gathers from this that somehow witches go on forever.

"Hover through the fog and filthy air" (l. 12) presents a chief image of *Macbeth*—darkness—and suggests that evil spirits are invisibly carrying witches in great numbers through the air. The Witches are "posters of the sea and land" (I.iii.33) and "made themselves air" (I.v.5). The Bleeding Sergeant of I.ii probably refers to this when he says that Macdonwald was a rebel because "the multiplying villainies of nature / Do swarm upon him."

This first scene of *Macbeth*, with its emphasis on *thunder*, *lightning*, and *darkness*, suggests that George Schaefer's filmed version of I.i was a mistake because in this the wasteland becomes the blue-skyed, bonny Scotland of the postcards and the calendars. At the end of the scene Polanski has two of the Witches diverge from the third in a V pattern intimating that these beings cover a wide sweep of earth.

ACT I, SCENE ii

Plot summary. This scene takes place in a military camp. The following characters enter: Duncan, king of Scotland; Malcolm, Duncan's elder son; Donalbain, Duncan's younger son; Lennox, a nobleman of Scotland; and attendants. They meet a wounded man referred to by Malcolm as "the sergeant." The Sergeant has been wounded apparently in the battle referred to by the Witches in the last scene, and Duncan decides that because the Sergeant has been wounded he must know how the fight has been going. We also learn from Duncan's remarks that the battle is part of a revolt against Duncan. Malcolm asks the Sergeant for news of the battle, and the wounded man tells this story. The fight was such that it was difficult to tell which side would win, the rebels' troops headed by Macdonwald or the forces loyal to Duncan, which, we learn in the course of the scene, are headed by Macbeth and Banquo. Added to Macdonwald's troops were Irish foot soldiers and horsemen ("kernes and gallowglasses"). Fortune seemed to be all on the rebels' side, but to no avail. For "brave Macbeth" despite fortune, made a passage for himself to Macdonwald by killing everyone between him and the leader of the rebels. When Macbeth came face to face with Macdonwald, he immediately ripped the rebel open from the navel to the lips, cut off his head, and placed it on the roof of the loyalists' castle.

Unfortunately, continues the Sergeant, that did not end the difficulties. No sooner did Macdonwald's Irish soldiers run away than the king of Norway, whose name is Sweno, in league with the rebels, took advantage of the situation, and "began a fresh assault," with new supplies of men and guns. But this did not make the loyalist leaders, Macbeth and Banquo, despair. They redoubled their strokes upon the enemy. As the Sergeant is about to continue, he finds he cannot, for he feels faint. When Duncan sends off the Sergeant to the doctor, Ross and Angus, two more noblemen of Scotland, enter. They have come from the battlefield, and Ross proceeds to finish the story broken off by the Sergeant's weakness. The king of Norway (referred to simply as "Norway") with his great number of troops was assisted by another traitor, the Thane of Cawdor. (Thane is a Scotch title approximating that of earl). Ross says the conflict was "dismal." However, the conflict was dismal only until "Bellona's bridegroom" (almost certainly meaning Macbeth) with equal strength met the strong king of Norway and beat him. Now Sweno, the king of Norway, wishes to come to terms with Duncan. Duncan says that the Thane of Cawdor will no longer deceive him, for Cawdor will be sentenced to death. And Macbeth, Duncan announces, will be the new Thane of Cawdor. Duncan sums up the situation in the last line, "What he [the Thane of Cawdor] hath lost, noble Macbeth hath won."

Critical analysis. The speeches of the Bleeding Sergeant, who is unnamed because Shakespeare wishes not to individualize him but to employ him as a spokesman, are in the Senecan tradition of the 1590s. A richer example is Shakespeare's account of "Aeneas' tale to Dido" in *Hamlet*, II.ii.472 ff. Similarities between the Sergeant's speeches and Senecan drama are: *slave* as a term of abuse, adjectives such as *direful* and *dismal*, the phrase "curbing his lavish spirit," and the personifications "Fortune" and "Bellona." J. M. Nosworthy thinks that Shakespeare was patronizing Senecan style.

This scene is now usually regarded as authentic Shakespeare, Nosworthy's "The Bleeding Captain Scene in *Macbeth*" having decisive influence; but *the faults remain* that caused some editors to regard I.ii as non-Shakespearean. *Bombast* is seen in the Sergeant's beginning three speeches with similes introduced by *as* (cf. Hamlet's "As's of great charge," V.ii.43). The bombast is dramatically functional, however, in that it provides contrast to the clear and unburdened speech of the King, which is just the kind of speech that James commended in *Basilikon Doron* to his son. Three of the Sergeant's speeches that should be worked into the rhetorical structure are set off in parentheses. L. 20 is a half line. L. 21 presents *which* with a doubtful antecedent. Ll. 20 and 22 both begin with *till*. There is no verb at the end of l. 26; so editors supply *break*. L. 38 in First Folio reads "So they doubly redoubled stroakes upon the foe"— twelve syllables instead of ten. The meter is faulty in ll. 50, 58–59. Ll. 7–9, which Holgar Norgaard thinks to be derivative from Daniel's *Cleopatra,* are puzzling.

The Sergeant regards Macdonwald as a compendium of human villainy because he is a rebel; on this account Macdonwald is assumed, in medieval fashion, to be stained with all vice. Rebellion against a lawful king in the *Mirror for Magistrates* and the Elizabethan *Homilies* was reckoned to be tantamount to rebellion against God. The introduction of Macdonald was topical inasmuch as James is on record as believing the Hebrideans to be utterly barbarous and averse to law, and in 1605 one Angus Macdonwald of the southern Hebrides rebelled against him. One should avoid reading into *Macbeth* suggestions of the glamor that since the eighteenth century has invested the Hebrides, what with the defeat of Prince Charles Stuart in 1745, the official subjugation of the clans, and the romanticizing of the Western Islands seen in Collins, Scott, Wordsworth, Keats, and other writers. The view of the Hebrideans held by James and reflected in *Macbeth* appears to have been usual in the earlier seventeenth century.

Is Duncan a coward? Some critics, such as Archibald Henderson, suggest that Duncan is guilty of cowardice in not taking part in the battle. Although, as Shakespeare conceives him, Duncan does not lack vigor, he is too old (V.i.45) to fight personally. He sees to it that his elder son takes part in the battle; and he is near the scene, not mewed up in a castle. Admittedly he asks the naive question, "Dismayed not this / Our captains, Macbeth and Banquo?" Certainly Shakespeare in preparing this play to be exhibited before James, who was descended from Duncan as well as Banquo, cannot be imagined, having offered incense to his sovereign at several places in the play, as intending to present a royal poltroon. One may note that Shakespeare changes Sweno from a Dane, as in Holinshed, into a Norwegian in deference to James's brother-in-law, King Christian of Denmark, present with James at the first performance of *Macbeth*.

Macbeth as butcher. The "bloody man" who is the Sergeant opens the play, John Holloway says imaginatively, "with an 'image of revolt,' the image of an actual deed of overturning, which serves from the start as emblem both of the central character, and of the course of the action." The Sergeant by his bloodiness foreshadows Malcolm's description of Macbeth as a "butcher," and ll. 22–23 anticipate bringing Macbeth's head onstage.

This scene presents some instances of the lesser carelessness of which Shakespeare was often guilty, perhaps cheerfully so. "Dollars" and "cannons" are mentioned—both anachronisms in the eleventh century. From Fife (I.ii.48) to Forres (I.iii.39) is about one hundred miles, an impossibly long way for the Bleeding Sergeant, and an instance of Shakespeare's indifference to details of Scottish geography.

ACT I, SCENE iii

Plot summary. The scene opens with the appointed meeting of the Three Witches. The First Witch gives an account of what she has been doing since their last meeting. She tells us that she has met a sailor's wife munching on chestnuts. When the Witch asked the wife for some nuts, the latter refused them to her. The

Witch will therefore soon take revenge, the revenge to be taken through the wife's husband, the sailor, who is the captain of the ship *Tiger*. She will cause the wind to blow so that he will never be able to sleep. He will be so weary that he will "dwindle, peak, and pine." However, the Witch, much as she can cause the captain of the *Tiger* to suffer, cannot make him lose his ship ("his bark").

The Witches then hear the sound of a drum, which announces the arrival of Macbeth and Banquo, who now enter. Macbeth's first words, spoken to Banquo, apparently comment on the weather, "So foul and fair a day I have not seen." They then see the Witches, who greet Macbeth with three titles, those of the Thane of Glamis, the Thane of Cawdor, and the future king. We learn from Banquo's speech immediately following the Witches' greeting that Macbeth is visibly shaken by the Witches' words, for Banquo says, "Good Sir, why do you start, and seem to fear / Things that do sound so fair?" But Macbeth is not only shaken; he is so involved with his thoughts that he does not hear Banquo and therefore does not answer Banquo's question. Returning to the Witches, Banquo asks them whether they have any predictions for his own future. They reply that he will be "lesser than Macbeth, and greater" and "not so happy, yet much happier." They also tell him that, although he himself will not be a king, he will be the father of kings. Macbeth, coming to himself, asks the Witches questions, but they vanish. As Macbeth and Banquo are speculating about the Witches, Ross and Angus enter to tell Macbeth that he has been granted the title of Thane of Cawdor. "The Thane of Cawdor lives," says Macbeth, "why do you dress me in borrow'd robes?" That is, Macbeth asks why the title should be given him when the man to whom it belongs is still alive. Macbeth is told the story of Cawdor's disloyalty; he then privately asks Banquo whether Banquo does not hope for the fulfillment of the prophecy for Banquo as the prophecy for Macbeth has in part been fulfilled. Banquo indicates a distrust for the Witches. He tells Macbeth that the tools of Satan ("instruments of Darkness") often fool us in the final result ("betray's in deepest consequence") by first telling us truths as thereby appearing honest.

As the other characters are involved in conversation, Macbeth speaks an aside. (An aside is a speech spoken by one character and heard by no one else on stage except those actors whom he may be addressing. In this case Macbeth is speaking to no other characters.) Macbeth tells himself that this beckoning him on (to greater things) by beings who know more than ordinary men ("supernatural soliciting") is ambiguous. That is, it is difficult to decide whether it is good or evil. The fact that he is made Thane of Cawdor seems to indicate that they tell the truth, and that appears to show that the beings are good. On the other hand, how can they be good when he allows himself to see a picture so horrible that it makes his hair stand on end and his heart beat unusually hard. Macbeth goes on to say that immediate dangers ("present fears") are less frightening to him than horrible things which he imagines. Exactly what makes his hair stand on end and heart beat wildly becomes a bit clearer in the following line: "My thought, whose murder is but fantastical . . . . " Apparently he has been thinking of murdering someone. The picture of himself as a murderer has been so vivid that he has been thoroughly shaken and caught up completely by his inner thoughts. He is incapable of seeing anything around him. Banquo remarks to his companions on Macbeth's self-absorption. But Macbeth continues his speech. If fortune ("chance") wants him to be king, he says, fortune may find a way to make him king. The implication is, of course, that Macbeth then will not have to do anything. (Almost certainly, he is thinking of the murder he has just been imagining.) Banquo still watching Macbeth remarks that Macbeth apparently is not yet accustomed to his new honors; they fit him "like our strange garments [which] cleave not to their mold." Macbeth ends his deliberations with "Come what come may, / Time and the hour runs through the roughest day." Banquo tells Macbeth that the group is waiting for him, and Macbeth begs their pardon. He also tells them that he appreciates the trouble they have taken to inform him of his good fortune. Then in an aside to Banquo, Macbeth advises Banquo to think about what has occurred, which they will sincerely discuss at their leisure. Banquo replies, "Very gladly."

Critical analysis. From l. 77 one gathers that this scene is set on a "blasted heath." The Witches, who seem more human in Act I than they will later, here speak among themselves in *headless octosyllabic couplets*, *i.e.*, in eight-syllabled lines that lack the first syllable and are rhymed in pairs.

> Weary sev' nights, nine times nine,
> Shall he dwindle, peak, and pine.
> Though his bark cannot be lost,
> Yet it shall be tempest-tost

This verse form differentiates them from the strictly human characters who speak mainly in unrhymed ten-syllabled lines called *blank verse*.

> If you can look into the seeds of time
> And say which grain will grow and
> which will not,
> Speak then to me, who neither beg
> nor fear
> Your favors nor your hate.

In their killing of the swine, the Witches behave like witches of English provenance. In their interest in affairs of state and in plotting the fall of kings, evident later in this scene, they are like Scottish witches; and they are therefore closer in conception to the witches of the continent, especially France. Line 7 may be a topical allusion: a *Tiger* sailed for the East in December 1604 with John Davis as master; many of the crew were killed by pirates, but the ship did manage to return to England. The rat of l. 9 is without a tail because Satan's creatures should not be so perfect as God's. We gather that the *Tiger* is fated to reach port and that *some things are beyond the powers of the Witches, a point suggesting Macbeth's freedom of the will*. The First

Witch, as Dennis Biggins observes, by the repetition of "do," a sexual euphemism, and by the assertion that she "will drain him [the sailor] dry as hay," is rendered in this instance as possessing one of the ordinary trappings of witchcraft. In ll. 35 ff. this coven of Witches ceremoniously adores their devils three times to each, intimating their mockery of the Trinity: *this is as far as Shakespeare ever goes in the depiction of devil-worship.* If Harpier, Graymalkin, and Paddock were physically present onstage, the scene would become more sinister because it would be more obviously idolatrous. Sir William Davenant's "improvement" of *Macbeth*, by making the Witches comic, made a dignified presentation of the title role more difficult for the great Thomas Betterton, the leading actor of Restoration London.

Sympathy between Witches and Macbeth. Then Macbeth and Banquo enter. Simon Forman, who saw *Macbeth* at the Globe in 1611, suggests that Macbeth appeared first on horseback, a piece of business unsupported by the Folio text. But since horses are restless and intimate nightmare, this action reflects Macbeth's state of mind. Furthermore, a horse indicates Macbeth's class as noble and as "Bellona's bridegroom," his interest in power. *In Polanski's filmed version the difficulty of distinguishing Macbeth from Banquo until the Witches address Macbeth enhances the ambiguity inherent in the play.* Since Macbeth and Banquo are marching from a double victory toward Forres with some of their troops (l. 30), we presume the troopers to be in the rear of the stage during the interview with the Weird Sisters. Macbeth says, "So foul and fair a day I have not seen," meaning that the weather is foul, and the victory is fair and, thematically, the ambiguity of appearances. Furthermore, *this line of Macbeth's suggests*, by its reminiscence of the Witches' "Fair is foul, and foul is fair," *a secret sympathy between Macbeth and the Witches before he has seen them.* With their repulsive beards, their choppy fingers, and their skinny lips, the Sisters are like English witches (Scottish witches could be beautiful), but Banquo's description in ll. 40–41 intimates their extraordinary dress. In the interview

Banquo appraises their appearance objectively whereas *Macbeth finds the Sisters secretly sympathetic to the baser instincts of his heart.* When the Witches speak, they oracularly announce; they do no "soliciting" (l. 130) by foretelling the murder of Duncan. If Macbeth is innocent of musing on opportunities of sending Duncan somewhat early to his Maker, one wonders why he starts with fear at the mention of a crown, and why, a little later (l. 139), he soliloquizes on murder. Hearing the prophecies does not in a practical sense remove Macbeth's free will, but in theory (since theory generally favors determinism) they do: *Shakespeare in any case* (unlike Chaucer) *was not interested in questions of free will and determinism.* The prophecy to Banquo "Thou shalt get kings" may certainly be regarded as *a topical allusion* what with King James in the first audience, since the Stuarts believed themselves to be descended from Banquo. Macbeth and Banquo receive the prophecies differently partly because Macbeth is announced by utter strangers to be Glamis and shortly becomes Cawdor, whereas the prophecies relating to Banquo pertain to the distant future after his death. In ll. 75–76 Macbeth is striving to discover whether the prophecies derive from good spirits or evil ones. He cannot learn this because the Witches exeunt—a business that should be managed without a trapdoor because they are linked to the Prince of the power of the air, *i.e.*, Satan, because the air over Scotland is filthy, and because Macbeth says (l. 81) they have vanished "into the air."

The question of Cawdor. We come now to consider the vexed matter of the Thane of Cawdor. Dr. Johnson wrote, "The incongruity of all the passages in which the Thane of Cawdor is mentioned is very remarkable": "Neither Ross knew what he had just reported, nor Macbeth knew what he had just done." Dugald Murdoch points out that a careful reading of the text reveals that Cawdor was not personally engaged in battle and that Macbeth did not fight him *vis-à-vis* in the field. Cawdor was a traitor, not a rebel. Furthermore, the text does not indicate that either Ross or Angus supervised Cawdor's execution. Murdoch thinks Cawdor's treason to have been purposely created to be opaque and thus a part of *Macbeth's* ambiguities. Daniel A. Amneus in "The Cawdor Episode in *Macbeth*" contends that the real difficulty (Murdoch disagrees) is Ross's ignorance in scene iii of what he knows in scene ii: the problem, he opines, lies in the time scheme; and he suggests that *scene ii, reconstructed from its confusion, would present sequentially*: a report by the Bleeding Sergeant on the first battle; a report (probably by Ross) of Sweno's landing at Fife; a report (in a new scene perhaps) of Cawdor's treachery; and a report of Macbeth's victory over Sweno.

Macbeth's "greater honor." Ross and Angus enter to convey the King's pleasure in Macbeth's prowess as demonstrated against the Hebridean rebels and the Norwegians. Ross says to Macbeth, "And for an earnest of a greater honor, / He bade me, from him, call thee Thane of Cawdor" (ll. 104–05). The "greater honor" must be the title "Prince of Cumberland." That would make Macbeth the succesor to the kingship, according to the *law of tanistry*, which permitted selection of the successor from *any* member of the "royal blood" line. (King James disapproved of tanistry; he preferred direct succession by the king's oldest son.)

But later King Duncan, perhaps forgetful of this promised "greater honor" for Macbeth, names his own son Malcolm as Prince of Cumberland! That gives Macbeth a motive for killing Duncan.

Of course, if Macbeth were to be named Prince of Cumberland, it would be unnecessary for him to undertake the murder of Duncan, and the complicity of Banquo in knowledge of the prophecy and of Macbeth's supposed intentions is removed, as Daniel Amneus has pointed out in "Macbeth's 'Greater Honor.'"

Some reasons to support this view are the following. In II.i.20–30 Banquo indicates willingness to cooperate with Macbeth and to win honor from him if Banquo can "still keep / My bosom franchis'd and allegiance clear": presumably he means that he will be "counsell'd" if Macbeth is to be named Prince of Cumberland. However, when Malcolm is given that title, and Duncan is dead, Banquo would be loyal to Malcolm. Another reason is that this supposition gives Macbeth a cause to decide against the murder; his proceeding with the regicide would be occasioned by Malcolm's unexpected accession to the title of Prince of Cumberland. A third reason is *Simon Forman's report of what he saw in the Globe performance* of *Macbeth* in 1611: "And Duncan bade them both kindly welcome and made Macbeth forthwith Prince of Northumberland [*i.e.*, Cumberland]." One point is certain: it is impossible to reconcile Macbeth's "greater honor" with Malcolm's being made heir apparent unless we know more than we do about Duncan's motivation. Scholars like A. C. Bradley, J. Q. Adams, and Dover Wilson have suspected omission, curtailment, or textual dislocation.

Macbeth, hearing himself addressed as Thane of Cawdor, replies, " . . . why do you thus dress me / In borrowed robes?" (ll. 108–09), preparing *the imagery*, discussed by Caroline Spurgeon, *of over-large clothing which Shakespeare employs as a visualization of Macbeth's tyranny.*

Macbeth's habit of repetition. Macbeth then in an aside (not a soliloquy because others are onstage) muses on the meaning of his being named Thane of Cawdor and wonders whether the *two* truths told him guarantee the truth of the *third* truth—that he is to be King of Scotland. *His language from l. 134 to l. 141 is remarkably unclear.* On the one hand, *he has reason to believe that he may honestly become king*: he is of royal blood, Duncan is old, the princes are young, Duncan has promised him "a greater honor" than Thane of Cawdor. On the other hand, these verses could mean that Macbeth has an inchoate intention of murdering Duncan even before Duncan nominates his successor: "My thought, whose murther yet is but fantastical," by employing bad grammar, suggests that Macbeth is in the process, as L. C. Knights observes, of forming his thought. "Smother'd in surmise" anticipates Lady Macbeth's "blanket of the dark" and Ross's choric comment in II.iv.6–10. *Here we see a habit of Macbeth which manifests itself when he is under pressure*, as Walter Gierasch has also remarked in II.ii.35–40; IV.i.144–48; V.iii.40–42; and V.v.9–15—*repetition by reformulation—"the hero's rhetoric in intense moments is characterized by saying a thing over again, usually three times."*

"The imperial theme" (l. 129) is a pregnant phrase that requires glossing. It did not suggest to the Jacobean audience an empire in the nineteenth-century sense. For the unschooled of that audience, *imperial* would probably have suggested Macbeth's hubristic imagination, *royal* being too weak a word for him. To the learned it might well call to mind, according to Henry N. Paul, the *Aeneid* as quoted in Gwinn's *Tres Quasi Sibyllae*, acted for King James's pleasure at Oxford on Aug. 27, 1605: "Imperium sine fine tuae, rex inclyte, stirpis" (rule of your dynasty without end, renowned king). In this association the line phrases the Stuart theme—the endless line of James's descendants (IV.i.117) and the imperial expansion of his country (IV.i.121). In the *Aeneid*, Jove promises to the descendants of Aeneas rule without bounds in time or space.

Macbeth ends the scene by excusing his fit, saying that his "dull brain was wrought / With things forgotten." The remark is improbable because it would be expected that his mind would be occupied with his new honor and its meaning.

ACT I, SCENE iv

Plot summary. We have here another short scene (58 lines) but one of great significance. Duncan, his two sons, Lennox, and some attendants enter. In the first two speeches we learn that the rebellious Thane of Cawdor has been executed. Malcolm tells us that a witness of the execution has reported that Cawdor confessed his treason and repented of it. He therefore died well:

"Nothing in his life / Became him like the leaving of it. . . ." Duncan talks of the difficulty of knowing from a man's face what is going on in his mind. Cawdor, Duncan says, "was a gentleman on whom I built / An absolute trust." He breaks off because Macbeth enters.

Banquo, Ross, and Angus enter with Macbeth. Duncan greets Macbeth with an elaborate speech, the essence of which is that Macbeth has done more for Duncan than Duncan can ever repay. Macbeth replies courteously and formally, saying in effect that the services that he, Macbeth, has given Duncan are their own reward and need no thanks from Duncan, for Macbeth owes these services to Duncan since Macbeth is a subject and Duncan a king. Macbeth states his reply thus in part: " . . . our duties / Are to your throne and state, children and servants," and Macbeth is only behaving properly "by doing everything / Safe toward [for the safety of] your love and honor."

Duncan now says, "I have begun to plant thee, and will labor / To make thee full of growing."

Duncan ends with: "let me infold thee, / And hold thee to my heart." That is, "Let me embrace you," which, of course, tells the actors what to do. Duncan says that his joys are so many that he is beginning to weep. Apparently when he recovers from weeping, he makes an important announcement. Malcolm, his eldest son, will hereafter have the title of Prince of Cumberland. But Malcolm will not be the only one newly honored. Other nobles will also receive greater honors. He then says that he will proceed to Inverness, Macbeth's castle. By becoming Macbeth's guest, he tells his host-to-be, he will put himself in even greater debt to Macbeth. Macbeth replies to Duncan, that he, Macbeth, will now put forth an effort which is not for Duncan's pleasure but for Macbeth's. Macbeth will hurry forth and he himself will be the messenger who will announce the news of Duncan's arrival, which will make Lady Macbeth, Macbeth's wife, "joyful." "My worthy Cawdor," says Duncan, thus at once thanking Macbeth and giving him permission to leave.

But before Macbeth exits, he has an aside. "The Prince of Cumberland!" he says, "that is a step / On which I must fall down, or else o'erleap. / For in my way it lies."

The reason Malcolm's becoming the Prince of Cumberland is an obstruction in Macbeth's way to the kingship is explained by George Steevens, the eighteenth-century Shakespearean scholar. "The crown of Scotland was originally not hereditary. When a successor was declared in the lifetime of a king, as was often the case, the title of Prince of Cumberland was immediately bestowed on him as the mark of his designation." Malcolm, therefore, in being given the title of Prince of Cumberland is being designated as the next king of Scotland. It is this obstruction that Macbeth must overcome.

Macbeth continues the aside by telling the stars to hide their light ("fires") so that their light will not discover Macbeth's "black and deep desires"; nor must their light show the eye shut in refusal to see [the action of] the hand. Yet he wants that deed to be done which, having been committed, the eye would be afraid to see.

After the speech Macbeth exits. During the speech Duncan had been talking with Banquo, and we hear the last part of their conversation. They have been apparently discussing and praising Macbeth, for Duncan agrees with Banquo that "he" is extremely brave. Duncan also says that when Macbeth is praised, Duncan is "fed." Commendations of Macbeth are "a banquet to me." And they exeunt to follow Macbeth. Duncan's last words are that Macbeth "is a peerless kinsman."

Critical analysis. Duncan is informed of the death of Cawdor. *His inability to judge Cawdor and Macbeth is not caused by senility.* Duncan, although often played as an old man, might be fifty. His mistakes are due, J. W. Draper thinks, to his sanguine humor—his physiological system has an excessive amount of blood: a defect of this kind of temperament is lack of caution to foresee and avoid pitfalls. There is some textual support for the view—Duncan weeps in this scene, tears being derived from blood; and in V.i Lady Macbeth will recall the incredible amount of blood that flowed from his aged body at the time of stabbing.

Macbeth, Banquo, Ross, and Angus enter. Duncan heaps praise on Macbeth not, as has been thought, to compensate him for naming Malcolm Prince of Cumberland, but out of the generosity of his nature. His repeated use of "thou" in addressing Macbeth (l. 16) is a sign of affection. The King's speech is so excessively laudatory that it might conceivably, as Edwin Thumboo notes, contribute something to Macbeth's self-esteem and want of regard for the proper relationship of king to thanes. Macbeth replies formally: his speech should not be delivered with histrionic hypocrisy that would distort the dramatic motive at this point even though it would provide (for some) "good theater." The King responds, "I have begun to plant thee, and will labor / To make thee full of growing." Critics often note that *the idea of planting is in the Bible usually associated with God, and the effect of the speech is to render Duncan sacrosanct, God's representative on earth.* In l. 37 Duncan shifts from *I* to *we*, signifying royal purpose and ceremony; and *he proceeds in a manner extraordinarily gauche* to declare Malcolm Prince of Cumberland. But the audience has now been prepared for Duncan's ineptitude, most notably seen in his misreading of Cawdor.

At this point there is conflict between the primary source and Shakespeare. Holinshed stated that the Scottish crown was not strictly hereditary, and that Macbeth, by the naming of Malcolm, had "a just quarrell so to doo [to kill Duncan] (as he tooke the matter). . . . " Shakespeare does not enlarge upon this hint and indeed, as Bradbrook says, suppresses notice of the *opposition between tanistry (an elective monarchy within the limits of the descendants of Macalpine) and the elective principle*, established by Malcolm Canmore. *The play emphasizes the hereditary principle to which James fondly referred in his speeches to Parliament and in his writings.* So Macbeth in

Shakespeare does not muse on the justice of his murder of Duncan. At the investiture of Malcolm it would be unwise for Macbeth to take or kiss the hand of the new heir apparent. Macbeth's aside in ll. 48–53 shows by the phrase "my black and deep desires" that the thought of murdering Duncan has become firm.

ACT I, SCENE v

Plot summary. The scene takes place at Macbeth's castle at Inverness. Lady Macbeth enters reading a letter from Macbeth. *The letter itself is the first piece of prose in the play.* Lady Macbeth's comments following the letter and the ensuing dialogue return to poetry. Lady Macbeth is reading apparently the last part of the letter. Macbeth has been writing her about the Witches, who, he says, met him on "the day of success," that is, the day of victory. He has learned dependably that they have more knowledge than ordinary mortals. Macbeth wanted very much to question them further, but they dissolved into air. As he "stood rapt in the wonder of it," the news came that he was the Thane of Cawdor, by which title the Witches had previously greeted him, and they also greeted him with "Hail, King that shalt be!" that is, hail, future king. Here the letter ends its account of his meeting with the Witches and addresses Lady Macbeth directly. This news of the meeting with the Witches, he thought it "good" to tell her so that her ignorance of her future greatness would not keep her from rejoicing at the prospect of her greatness ("that thou might'st not lose the dues of rejoicing, by being ignorant of what greatness is promised thee"). Immediately before the last remark Macbeth calls Lady Macbeth his "dearest partner of greatness." He ends by telling his wife to put the letter to her heart, and he bids her farewell.

Lady Macbeth now comments on the letter. She says that Macbeth shall attain the goal he has been promised, that is, the kingship. But she is afraid that his character is "too full o' the

milk of human kindness, / To catch the nearest way." She
continues by saying that although he is ambitious, he does not
have that evil in his character that will permit him to reach his
great goal: " . . . what thou wouldst highly, / That wouldst thou
holily." Then, as though she were addressing him directly, she
says, "Hie thee hither. . . ." She wants him to come quickly so
that she can fill him with her spirit and disperse with a tongue-
lashing all of his character which prevents him from attaining
the crown ("the golden round") promised him by fate and
supernatural help ("metaphysical aid").

A Messenger interrupts Lady Macbeth's thoughts to inform her
that the king will arrive at Inverness that night. "Thou'rt mad to
say it," cries Lady Macbeth. Would not Macbeth, who is with
the king, have warned them beforehand so that the castle could
be prepared for the king's arrival? The Messenger replies that
one of his fellow servants had indeed been sent beforehand and
is completely out of breath from rushing with the news. He
precedes Macbeth, who will arrive before Duncan. When the
Messenger leaves, Lady Macbeth has a soliloquy of some
fifteen lines. In the first line and one-half she imagines a raven
greeting the "fatal" arrival of Duncan to her castle ("my battlements"). She says that a raven greeting this arrival would have
a voice even more harsh than usual (obviously because the
entrance will be "fatal" to Duncan). She then invokes (calls on
for aid) "Spirits / That tend on mortal thoughts. . . ." That is, she
asks the spirits that are the servants of murderous ("mortal")
thoughts to come to her aid. She wants them to "unsex" her, that
is, to take away her womanliness, which makes her soft-hearted.
And she wants these spirits to fill her from head to toe with the
worst sort of cruelty. She wants the spirits to make it so that
nothing in her nature will prevent her from carrying out her
"fell" (cruel) purpose, She continues the invocation, "Come to
my woman's breasts. . . ." She now wishes the servants of
murderous thoughts (whom she this time calls "murdering
ministers") to act as her children sucking at her breasts. But
instead of taking milk from her breasts as children normally
would, the "murdering ministers," she hopes, will take milk and

inject in its place gall (bitterness). She now invokes "thick night" and tells night to cover itself with the gloomiest smoke of hell. She wants this done so that her knife (she means, of course, the eye that is guiding her knife) will not see the wound it makes and heaven will not be able to peep through the dark to tell her to stop.

The entrance of Macbeth brings us to the first dialogue between the play's two main characters. Lady Macbeth greets her husband with his two current titles, Glamis and Cawdor. He will have a title, she continues, greater than both in the future. His letters have made her feel the future in this moment. She obviously means that she feels now like the queen. Macbeth replies with a statement that apparently does not follow logically, "My dearest love / Duncan comes here tonight." Lady Macbeth asks her husband when Duncan is leaving, and he replies, "Tomorrow, as he purposes [intends]." Her response is that the sun will never see the morning (when Duncan leaves their castle). Macbeth apparently looks disturbed at his wife's remark, for she says, "Your face, Thane, is as a book, where men / May read strange matters." Then in a series of images which mean more or less the same she advises him not to give away his thoughts by the expression on his face: "To beguile [cheat] the time [that is, the men of the time], / Look like the time . . . / . . . look like the innocent flower, / But be the serpent under't." She adds ironically, "He that's coming / Must be provided for [prepared for]. . . ." She concludes by saying that he shall turn over to her the management of the affair, the results of which shall give to the rest of their days "sovereign sway and masterdom." Macbeth answers only, "We will speak further." She tells him again to keep a face that indicates an undisturbed mind, "Only look up clear . . . ." To change one's face (an indication of disturbance in the mind) is always to be afraid. Lady Macbeth ends by saying, "Leave all the rest to me."

Critical analysis. Lady Macbeth reads a letter from Macbeth which—being composed between I.iii and I.iv—gives no intelligence of the King's purpose to visit Macbeth's castle and no notice of Malcolm's being named Prince of Cumberland. Macbeth, in short, has not at that point consciously determined to kill Duncan. Lady Macbeth should not read the letter in the manner of a fiend lest it spoil the contrast between her present mood and the black mood that develops later in the scene. She does not burn, as Holinshed says, "in unquenchable desire to beare the name of a queene"; but since Macbeth writes "that thou mightest not lose the dues of rejoicing by being ignorant of what greatness is promis'd thee," we gather that being Queen of Scotland is quite to her taste. By employing the correct name for the Witches, *i.e.*, "weird sisters," Macbeth suggests that he has learned something by investigation. They said to him, "Hail, King that shalt be." "Shalt be," Lady Macbeth thinks, does not mean determination in the full sense of the word because Macbeth is only a murderer in his thought-life, a hypocrite, and a man whose conscience is almost exclusively prudential. When Lady Macbeth says that he is "too full o' th' milk of human kindness / To catch the nearest way," she means that although he would assuredly enjoy the fruits of killing Duncan, *i.e.*, the crown, his nature is averse to the unnatural act of regicide, and his imagination is burdened with thoughts of the horror with which his compatriots would view a king-killing tyrant. Lady Macbeth habitually refers to the killing of Duncan in *periphrasis* (or roundabout speech), *e.g.*, "the nearest way," because she shrinks from the bloody deed itself; nevertheless, *unlike Macbeth, she is ruthless in pursuit of ambition, and she promises to goad him into achieving by direct action (rather than by awaiting) what has been promised him.*

When the Messenger enters to give news on Duncan's intention to stay the night, Lady Macbeth in a soliloquy invites "spirits" to "unsex" her and fill her "topful / Of direst cruelty." *If she is depicted as young and attractive*, as in Polanski's filmed version, *this line has more meaning than if she is played as a middle-aged, "bitchy," hatchet-faced woman: it underlines the theme of fair on the outside, foul within. The usual view of the speech*, as seen in the Variorum edition—John Dover Wilson, George L. Kittredge, and W. C. Curry—is that she is inviting demon-possession. *A contrary view*, expressed by Paul H. Kocher, is that "the spirits that tend on mortal thoughts" are animal spirits that communicate the mind's decisions to the body. Thick melancholy blood, reinforced by fresh supplies of melancholy from the spleen, would thus flow towards the heart and make it colder and heavier. By this means the pronouncements of conscience drawn from its reading of the engraved moral law of nature ("compunctious visitings of nature") will be blocked from the will and from bodily organs that would put them into effect. In this state the other kind of nature ("nature's mischief"), meaning the corrupt passions of fallen mankind unpurified by divine grace, is to predominate. *Another view*, advanced by Alice Fox, is that "visitings of nature" was commonly euphemistic for menstruation, and that Lady Macbeth uses blocked menses, causing thick and gross blood, as a metaphor for a blocked conscience.

Demon possession. The idea of demon possession better suits the atmosphere of *Macbeth* and the predilections of King James. On the other hand, ll. 43–47 lend color to Kocher's interpretation because here Lady Macbeth, contrary to the Christian position, takes a purely materialistic view of conscience, as something, that is, that can be stifled by thickened blood; and in this way of thinking she may be likened to Iago and Edmund. Lady Macbeth asks the demons or animal spirits to exchange her woman's milk for gall—a line that, one thinks, interested James because of his belief, common in the time, that the morals of nurses affected their babies through milk. James attributed his Protestantism (his mother was a Roman Catholic) to his nurse, Helen Litell. Lady Macbeth concludes the soliloquy by invoking night to invest the projected murder with "the dunnest smoke of hell."

Incidentally, *peep* in l. 53 was not in 1606 a word with comic overtones as today.

Macbeth enters not knowing that his wife has learned of Duncan's coming. One notices that Lady Macbeth's "the all-hail hereafter" (I.v.55) is like the Third Witch's greeting to Macbeth in I.iii.50, from which we gather an obscure connection between Lady Macbeth's present mood and the Witches. "All hail" to Shakespeare is enriched by reminiscence of Judas's kiss in the Gospels (*III Henry VI*.V.vii.33; *Richard II*.IV.i.169). An illustration of how acting can bring *Macbeth* to life is observed in the actor Edmund Kean's employing a pause and stress in l. 60—"Tomorrow, as he ... purposes"—to suggest that the idea of killing Duncan at Dunsinane has already occurred to Macbeth. Lady Macbeth now begins to chastise Macbeth with the valor of her tongue, counseling him in a line suggesting the story of Adam and Eve, "look like th' innocent flower, / But be the serpent under't." She never tries to banish the thought of killing Duncan, and she never thinks of an alternative. Her utterance of l. 70—"Give solely sovereign sway and masterdom"—has a roll that somehow conveys the juicy, full-blooded relish that she takes in the thought of being translated to the crown.

ACT I, SCENE vi

Plot summary. The scene occurs in front of the castle at Inverness. Duncan and his party enter. The characters in the party whose presence interests us are Malcolm and Donalbain (Duncan's two sons), Banquo, Lennox, Macduff, Ross, and Angus, all of whom are Scottish noblemen, or thanes. The scene is a formal one consisting in large part of the elaborate and courteous language used in ceremony, in this case the ceremony of greeting the arrival of a guest. Here, of course, it is a special guest, the king. When Duncan enters, he remarks upon the pleasantness of the air around Macbeth's castle. Banquo agrees with Duncan by saying that the presence of a martlet's nest in every possible corner of the face of the castle proves that "the heaven's breath / Smells wooingly here," that is, that the air smells enticingly here. The presence of so many martlets' nests shows the air's pleasantness because the martlet is "temple-haunting." That is, the martlet ordinarily nests in churches. If he chooses to rest elsewhere, it is because the air is as soft and pleasing as the air about the churches. Banquo ends his speech by saying that he has observed that where "they most bred" the air is "delicate," that is, soft.

Lady Macbeth enters, and Duncan greets her in an elaborate and complicated way. The point of the speech is that Lady Macbeth really does not mind the extra pains she takes in having Duncan as a guest, because she loves Duncan. Lady Macbeth replies as elaborately as Duncan has spoken. She says that double all of the service which Macbeth and Lady Macbeth have done for Duncan does not compare to the "honors deep and broad" which Duncan has given their house. For both the old honors and the recent honors Macbeth and Lady Macbeth will pray to God for him ("We rest your hermits"). Duncan asks for Macbeth, who, he says, has ridden faster than Duncan. Duncan had hoped to precede Macbeth. Duncan concludes with "Fair and noble hostess, / We are your guest tonight." The hostess replies that everything in the house is really Duncan's. He asks her to conduct him to Macbeth, whom he loves and whom he will continue to honor; and they exeunt.

Critical analysis. Banquo, we gather, has declined to tell Duncan of what he and Macbeth have heard from the Sisters and of what he may suspect concerning Macbeth. It would, after all, be embarrassing for Banquo—since his descendants are to inherit the crown, according to the prophecy—to speak to the King in this sense. One may also say that Banquo has no occasional motive to be thus confidential with the King inasmuch as, although he appears to be as worthy as Macbeth, he is not rewarded with the thaneship of Cawdor or any other material honor or title.

There is *tragic irony, the kind for which Sophocles is famous*, in Duncan's remark "The air / Nimbly and sweetly recommends itself / Unto our gentle senses" because nowhere is Scottish air more infected, though sightlessly, than at Macbeth's castle. The hill air, sweet and fresh, contrasts with "the blanket of the dark," and suggests in its hospitality to martlets (house *martins* or swallows) that Duncan, too, is born from Heaven.

Banquo's speech on martins (ll. 33 ff.) is pregnant with dramatic significance: it continues the irony of the King's first speech; it contrasts a temple to Macbeth's bloody hall; it exhibits the composure of Duncan and Banquo; it juxtaposes martins and the ravens on the battlements; and it points up an ironic difference between the martins' "procreant cradle" and the childlessness of the Macbeths (and almost all other villains in Shakespearean drama). Martins were traditionally supposed to know when a house was on the verge of some great collapse and to leave it. Peter M. Daly says, "By not abandoning the castle Banquo's martlets ironically underscore the theme of deception; they reflect in the world of nature the human misreading of the situation."

Lady Macbeth's hypocrisy. It is better dramatically for Lady Macbeth to greet Duncan first, for she is at this stage a better actor than Macbeth. *Duncan's speech (ll. 10–14) is thus paraphrased by Henry N. Paul:* "The modest Duncan dislikes the pomp and ceremony of a royal visit. The visit is therefore a 'trouble' to both the host and the royal guest. But it is also the means by which both show their love. Therefore, the king thanks his host for his trouble, because showing love, and so teaches his host to thank the king for his trouble for the same reason." Paul makes the point that the King finds the royal "we" troublesome. Lady Macbeth responds with gratitude for the honors the King has done her house, concluding "We rest your ermites." *In this piece of arrant hypocrisy she alludes to Duncan's preceding religious adjuration and resorts to the hyperbole of describing herself and Macbeth as religious hermits praying in solitude for Duncan's welfare.*

Of the scene as a whole Sir Joshua Reynolds wrote in his *Eighth Discourse at the Royal Academy*, "The subject of this quiet and easy conversation gives that repose so necessary to the mind, after the tumultuous bustle of the preceding scenes, and perfectly contrasts the scene of horrour that immediately succeeds." Sir Joshua failed to note that horror is increased by Duncan's cheerful confidence amidst the scene of his impending doom.

ACT I, SCENE vii

Plot summary. The scene opens with servants serving the dinner in honor of Duncan's visit. Macbeth enters and speaks a soliloquy, which begins, "If it were done when 'tis done, the 'twere well / It were done quickly...." *It*, of course, refers to the murder. He continues in a series of images the essence of which is: If the murder should be successful here on this earth and have no dangerous consequences, the risk of punishment in the next world would be worth it. But in cases such as the murder of Duncan, Macbeth goes on to say, we are sentenced for our crime in this life. The sentence is this: when we commit an assassination, we in effect teach others to commit the same act. It is "even-handed justice." Macbeth now turns from the practical reasons why he should not kill Duncan to the moral reasons. He says that Duncan is in his house "in double trust." First, Macbeth is both Duncan's relative and Duncan's subject. Both of these ties to Duncan make the murder reprehensible. Second, Macbeth is Duncan's host; as Duncan's host Macbeth should shut the door against Duncan's murderer, not carry the murder knife himself. Macbeth goes on to a political reason why he should not murder Duncan. Duncan, he says, has been so mild and guiltless as king that Duncan's virtues will cry out like a trumpet against his murder ("taking-off"). And pity, as though it were "a naked new-born babe," or some member of an order of angels ("heaven's cherubins") riding the wind, "Shall blow the horrid deed in every eye"; there will then be a tremendous amount of weeping ("tears shall drown the wind"). Macbeth continues with an image from horsemanship, which says he has no reason to murder Duncan except ambition.

Lady Macbeth interrupts Macbeth's thoughts with her entrance. We learn that Duncan has almost finished supper and that he has wondered why Macbeth has disappeared from the table. Macbeth then says that he and his wife will no longer continue with the business of killing Duncan. The reason is that Duncan has recently honored Macbeth, and Macbeth has "bought / Golden opinions from all sorts of people, / Which would be worn now in their newest gloss, / Not cast aside so soon." At Macbeth's remarks Lady Macbeth pours out a torrent of contempt, the main idea of which is this: you do not really love me when you are not man enough to go out and get what you want. Macbeth replies, "I dare do all that may become [is appropriate to being] a man. . . ." To this his wife says, "What beast was't, then, / That made you break this enterprise to me?" That is, as she explains in the next line, when you dared to plan the murder, you were a man; so that if you dare do all that is appropriate to being a man, you would dare do the murder. By breaking the promise to commit the deed you are behaving like a creature lower than a man, which is a beast. She goes on to say that when Macbeth promised her to kill Duncan the best possible occasion for the murder had not presented itself ("Nor time, nor place, / Did then adhere") and in fact he had said that he would have created a good occasion for the deed. But now that the best possible occasion has presented itself, he is unmanned. She then follows with *one of the most blood-curdling images the of play*. She knows, she says, "How tender 'tis to love the babe that milks me [feeds at my breast]." But rather than break the kind of promise that Macbeth wants to break now, she would, while the baby at her breast was smiling up at her, pull her nipple from the baby's mouth and crush out the baby's brains. Macbeth has no answer to this and turns to the practical problem of possible failure. Lady Macbeth tells him that as long as he has courage, they will not fail. She then recounts the plan for the murder. When

Duncan is sound asleep, as he will be after his hard day of travel, she will so fill with drink his bedroom attendants that they will sleep as though they were dead. Then Macbeth and his wife can do anything they wish to Duncan, who will be unwatched. And they can put the guilt upon the drunken ("spongy") guards. Macbeth says that his wife ought to bear only boys because her courageous spirit should go into the making of men. He then turns back to the murder plan and, as though he had not heard his wife's last words, he repeats in the form of a question what she had said about the guilt being put upon Duncan's drunken attendants. She replies that since she and Macbeth would be loudly grief-stricken over Duncan's death, no one would dare put the blame anywhere but on the drunken attendants. Macbeth says that he has decided to go through with the deed. And now Macbeth repeats his wife's advice of a previous scene: the expression on the face must be innocent although the heart intends murder.

Critical analysis. While Duncan and the others are dining, Macbeth muses alone on the heinousness of killing the King, but this is perhaps not the first time such thoughts have circulated in his head. Lady Macbeth, upon reading his letter, immediately assumed that Duncan would be murdered. As soon as Macbeth met her, he knew what was in her mind. Later in scene vii Lady Macbeth will state that Macbeth swore to carry out such a murder, and this swearing occurred when there was neither time nor place for it: Macbeth would make time and place. On the other hand, Macbeth is violently shaken when he thinks of the murder; and *Shakespeare does not make this point quite clear* to the audience although he might have done so in I.iii. If Macbeth harbored before the beginning of the play the idea of killing Duncan, the play would be something nearer melodrama than it is.

According to Paul, what happens is this: Duncan was incompetent to control his rebellious subjects. Macbeth offered his services *in propria persona* to crush this rebellion (I.iii.91). His pride grew in this work, and he offered his wife the thought that

because of Duncan's ineptitude he should be disposed of
(I.vii.48). Lady Macbeth embraced the thought, but Macbeth
put it away because it amounted to "murder" (I.iii.139) and
therefore involved his own damnation (I.vii.20).

*Modern criticism, however, generally cannot credit the idea
that a man like this would commit so great a crime and therefore
sees Macbeth as diseased from the start of the play.* Macbeth
delivers the opening soliloquy not as if he had made up his mind:
he is debating here. The first line thus means that if it were ended
when it is performed, it would be well. Macbeth does not
dismiss the thought of judgment in another world as if it were
a chimera; he entertains it as a possibility that he is willing to risk
in the interest of his worldly ambition. He argues that he should
not kill the King because of prudence, loyalty (kinship, allegiance, hospitality), and pity. But if one looks hard at pity,
which from its position should constitute the climax of his
argument, one finds, à la Cleanth Brooks, that the pity that
influences Macbeth is the pity of the public for their murdered
king.

Naked babes and the four horsemen. Lines 21 ff. thus mean
that pity, when born, is helpless as a babe; but when blown into
many hearts, it becomes stronger than the wind. Grover Smith
suggests that Shakespeare may have been influenced by emblematic naked infants fast riding the wind over the ocean
spaces of decorated Renaissance maps. S. R. Swaminathan
thinks that a Flemish *Book of Hours*, owned by Henry VIII,
might have relevance inasmuch as the human soul at death is
"symbolized by a naked infant in an oval glory." This point has
color in the quasi-universality of the motif. " . . . or heaven's
cherubin, hors'd / Upon the sightless couriers of the air / Shall
blow the horrid deed in every eye." Whether the invisible
"cherubin" are powerful angels or tender babes (on this debate
see Grover Smith), these lines, Holloway assures us, would
have reminded the first audiences of the Four Horsemen of the
Apocalypse (Rev. 6, 2–8), "bringing, as they ride over the earth,
the disasters which are the proper result of, proper retribution

for, human evil." In short, Macbeth's conscience counsels him to fear the consequences of sin rather than to love the fruits of righteousness. Although active, his conscience is not altogether admirable, for it is negative in the guidance it gives him. *So he begins his course of evil with complete knowledge of what he is doing and with the evident willingness to exchange a heavenly crown (Rev. 2, 10) for an earthly one. He is deceived by the prophecies of the Witches, but he is not deceived by them into believing that evil is good or that evil is beautiful.*

Sexual blackmail. When Lady Macbeth enters full of determination to dispatch Duncan this night, and Macbeth proves averse in order to enjoy the "golden opinions" he has won, Shakespeare exploits the contrast between a feminine-looking woman with great strength of will and a masculine-looking man with a sufficiency of courage but with feminine fancy and weak resolution. In saying "From this time / Such I account thy love" (ll. 38–39), Lady Macbeth goads her husband with something like sexual blackmail. She parallels Macbeth's unwillingness to kill the King with sexual nonperformance. The upshot of all this, as Dennis Biggins points out, is that Shakespeare metaphorically identifies Macbeth's impulse to murder with perverted sexual passion. She chides him with cowardice, alluding to the proverb that "the cat would eat fish but would not wet her feet." As Eugene Waith has pointed out, Lady Macbeth's conception of manhood emphasizes valor and resolution but excludes moral purpose: in the Renaissance word she identifies masculinity with *virtù*, and, of course, fantasizes dreadfully about what it is to be a man. To pump courage into Macbeth, she tells of her willingness to dash out the brains of her nurseling if she had sworn as he had done. For those who (with some reason) believe that Shakespeare shrinks from the horrible, one may point out that Ovid has an account, as James Wood notes, of a mad father, Athamas, who brains his child; so Shakespeare may have borrowed this repulsive conception.

Whether Lady Macbeth had a child is a vexed critical question. We simply do not know. One may say in passing that in

Shakespeare's plays, persons of villainous inclinations (except Aaron in *Titus Andronicus*) do not have children; and although Macbeth and Lady Macbeth must often attempt to have a child, for Macbeth's ambition is dynastic more than personal, they never succeed. *The language of the play*, as Alice Fox has especially noted, *is much concerned with pregnancy, miscarriage, normal and abortive births*.

Macbeth asks, "If we should fail?" *Lady Macbeth's response* "We fail" *should be followed by a question mark rather than an exclamation point*, for her sense is "How can we fail? If only you act resolutely we cannot fail." Taking a figure from the crossbow, she advises him to "screw your courage to the sticking place." Ernest Schanzer, taking *warder* in l. 65 to be a misprint for "warden," as against Kittredge, paraphrases ll. 64–67 thus: "The full meaning of the image is therefore that the receptacle which should collect only the pure drops of reason, the final distillate of the thought process, will be turned into the retort in which the crude undistilled liquids bubble and fume." In this elaborate figure Lady Macbeth explains how soporific wine will put Duncan's chamberlains into "swinish sleep" and permit both the murder of the King and the assumption of their guilt for regicide. Thus Lady Macbeth, sketching the practical details of the murder, changes her lord's reluctance to enthusiasm for the deed.

ACT II, SCENE i

Plot summary. The scene is still Macbeth's castle at Inverness, this time, the stage directions tell us, a court of the castle. Banquo is talking with his son, Fleance. We learn from their first lines that the night is dark. "There's husbandry in heaven"; says Banquo as a mild joke, "Their candles are all out." He means there must be economy in heaven because the lights of heaven (the stars) are shut off. Banquo goes on to say that, although he is very tired, he does not want to sleep because of the "cursed thoughts," that is, bad dreams, he has in his sleep. Apparently because he hears someone coming, he asks Fleance for his sword. With his sword in hand he shouts, "Who's there?" Macbeth enters and answers, "A friend." Banquo wonders why Macbeth is not yet asleep. The king, Banquo says, has already gone to bed having had "unusual pleasure," and he has bestowed many gifts in Macbeth's servants' quarters ("your offices"). Banquo also shows Macbeth a diamond that Duncan has left for Lady Macbeth because she has been such a "kind hostess." And, Banquo says, Duncan is "shut up in measureless content," that is, has concluded the day with a satisfaction so great that it cannot be measured. Macbeth says courteously that he and his wife were unprepared, and therefore they could not do as much for the king as they would have liked. Banquo then tells Macbeth that he dreamt last night of the "three weird sisters," whose predictions have partially come true for Macbeth. The latter replies, "I think not of them. . . ." However, he continues, Banquo and he, when they have leisure and if Banquo wishes to give the time, might talk about the matter. Banquo agrees. Macbeth goes on, "If you shall cleave to my consent, when 'tis, / It shall make honor for you." That is, if you go along with me when the time comes, you will be rewarded. Banquo picks up the word *honor* from Macbeth's remark and uses it first in another one of its senses. (Actually, he does not use the word *honor*; rather he uses *none* in reference to Macbeth's using the word, and Banquo means, no *honor*.) He changes its meaning from *reward* (Macbeth's usage) to *honorableness*, or *uprightness*. Banquo's reply, therefore, signifies: As long as I lose no uprightness in trying to add to my rewards ("it" referring to *honor*) and keep myself guiltless and innocent. I shall listen to you. They wish each other good night, and Banquo and Fleance leave.

Macbeth is left alone with his servant to whom he gives instructions for Lady Macbeth. She is to ring a bell when his "drink" (his bedtime drink, his nightcap) is ready. Left alone, he speaks another soliloquy. "Is this a dagger, which I see before me, / The handle toward my hand?" He thinks he sees a dagger in the air, the handle toward him. He wishes to take hold of the dagger, but since it is an hallucination, he cannot do so. He sees it still as vividly as the one which he now actually draws. He asks himself whether it is real or a creature of his mind, and he says that it leads him the way that he was going (that is, to murder Duncan). And the dagger he sees in the air is the very one he was going to use for the murder. Now he can see drops of blood on the dagger. "There's no such thing," he cries. "It is the bloody business which informs / Thus to mine eyes." That is, there is no such dagger in the air; the fact that I am going to do the murder ("the bloody business") causes me to imagine I see it. Macbeth goes on to give his impression of the atmosphere of the night. He says that over half the world all activity seems to have stopped, and evil dreams are disturbing sleep. Witches are celebrating the rites of the moon ("Hecate," another name for Diana, the goddess of the moon; but Hecate was considered also the goddess of witchcraft). And "withered murder," that is, murder personified as wrinkled and shrunken, awakened by his guard, the wolf, strides secretly and quietly toward his purpose, like Tarquin. (Tarquin is Sextus Tarquinius, the son of the last Roman king. Tarquin's rape of the virtuous Lucrece caused the expulsion of his family from Rome and the establishment of the Roman republic.) Macbeth then addresses the stones of the earth asking them not to make noise as he walks, for the noise will take from the current occasion the horror which is appropriate to it. The bell sounds which Macbeth had the servant tell Lady Macbeth to ring. Apparently, it is a pre-arranged signal between them, the signal which summons Duncan to heaven or to hell. That is, it is the signal that tells Macbeth that he is to murder Duncan.

Critical analysis. In this scene Shakespeare first exploits the *contrasts between Banquo's self-control and Macbeth's bloody thoughts*; then he emphasizes the *contrasts between Macbeth's public manner and his private aims, between the ceremony due him as a king and his unworthy self.* The poet departs from Holinshed's implication of Banquo in the conspiracy *because*, if he did not so, the King's ancestor would be guilty of treason, *because* James believed that rebellion is never justified, even against a wicked king, and *because* the story would then be lacking in inward conflict. Banquo and Fleance prepare themselves for sleep. From Banquo's removal of his weapons (ll. 4–5 contain implicit stage directions) we gather that everyone feels safe in the castle. Incidentally, Shakespeare's explicit stage directions are sparse by comparison with modern practice: this means that actors have more freedom of interpretation in Shakespearean plays. Banquo now prays for grace against "the cursed thoughts that nature / Gives way to in repose," a remark both general and particular in application. Banquo is presumably praying that God will restrain in him thoughts of hastening the day when his issue will become kings.

Macbeth enters, and Banquo delivers to him a diamond, a gift of Duncan to Lady Macbeth, which Banquo has about him undelivered—*seemingly hasty writing on Shakespeare's part*. Banquo, curiously, tells Macbeth, "I dreamt last night of the three weird sisters," yet *it cannot be shown how a night passes between the first appearance of the Sisters and the night spent by Banquo at Macbeth's castle*. Macbeth lies in response, "I think not of them." Then, assuming *the royal "we"* (l. 22) in anticipation, he apparently thinks of awarding honors to his supporters. If Macbeth is made king, Banquo can expect to move up the ladder, perhaps to become Thane of Cawdor. Banquo promises to be receptive to Macbeth's overtures so long as they are within the eye of honor.

How actors "handle" the "dagger." Banquo and Fleance leaving, Macbeth begins hallucinating about the dagger and uttering a soliloquy. It would be dramatically better for Macbeth to view the dagger at first slowly and reluctantly, struggling with belief that it is there and with diminishing skepticism that it is not there. *The best actors*—Garrick, Macready, Irving, and Booth—*did not use daggers onstage because they were able to make the audience see and feel what was not there*. The dramatic critic of the *Daily News*, Sept. 21, 1875, wrote of Irving: "We believe it has always been customary in the dagger scene to confront the audience looking upwards, as if the imaginary dagger was hovering in the air somewhere between the performer and the audience. Mr. Irving on the contrary sees the dagger at a much lower point as he follows it across the stage, drawn as it were by its fascination toward the arched entrance to the chamber of the king—a fine point being his averted hands as if the man 'infirm of purpose,' and conscious of the spell that is around and about him, could not trust himself to clutch the airy weapon save in words." The dagger is Macbeth's imagination leading him on, and his imagination is the fruit of his desires. In ll. 49–60 he allies himself with the wolf, suggesting his intention to destroy the lamb (God), and with less point he likens himself to Tarquin, who was, as Irving Ribner says, "the destroyer of chastity, symbolic in the Renaissance of the perfection of God." Macbeth then goes offstage to murder Duncan. Polanski, unlike Shakespeare, exhibits Macbeth in the act of killing Duncan; while this notable effusion is occurring, the crown rolls from a table to a floor suggesting, again unlike Shakespeare, that its slipperiness will continue to attract ambition beyond the confines of the play.

ACT II, SCENE ii

Plot summary. The setting is the same as in the previous scene. The beginning of this scene occurs as Macbeth is in Duncan's room committing the murder. Lady Macbeth enters in a state of high excitement. In the last scene of Act I she had said that with "wine and wassail" she was going to make Duncan's two attendants drunk. Apparently, she has not only done so, but she has also taken some of the drink herself, for she says when she enters, "That which had made them drunk hath made me bold. . . ." But despite the daring given her by drink, she is nervous. "Hark!" she cries when she hears a sound, which turns out to be nothing but the shriek of an owl. "He is about it," she then says; that is, Macbeth is committing the murder. She recounts her preparations: the doors are open (so that Macbeth can get in); the attendants ("grooms") are snoring, for she has drugged their nightcaps ("possets"). Macbeth suddenly cries from inside, "Who's there?" Lady Macbeth is afraid that Macbeth's shout means that the grooms have awakened and that the murder has not been committed. The attempt at the deed, she says, not the murder itself will cause their failure. She grows increasingly nervous. She thinks she hears a noise again, for she cries once more, "Hark!" She must now be thinking that Macbeth cannot find the daggers she had prepared: she says, "I laid their daggers ready; / He could not miss 'em." Then she says, "Had he not resembled / My father as he slept, I had done't." At this point Macbeth enters, and his wife calls to him, "My husband!"

When Macbeth enters, he tells his wife that he has "done the deed." But they are both obviously nervous, for they ask each other a series of quick questions about noises they have heard. The exchange ends with Macbeth's "Hark!" and they both apparently listen, hearing nothing. Then Macbeth asks who was sleeping in the "second chamber," that is, the bedroom behind Duncan's. "Donalbain," Lady Macbeth replies. Macbeth apparently looks at his bloody hands, for he says, "This is a sorry sight." His wife tells him that he is foolish to think so. Macbeth then goes on to recall an incident that occurred while he was in Duncan's chamber. In telling of the incident Macbeth talks of two men who were sleeping in a room. It is difficult to know whether he is talking of Malcolm and Donalbain who were apparently sleeping in the room behind Duncan or the two grooms who were in Duncan's room. It hardly matters which of the two groups he is talking about. It is the story that Macbeth tells that counts, not the participants. In any case, one of the men laughed in his sleep and the other cried out, "Murder!" The sounds each made woke the other, but they said their prayers and returned to sleep. During their prayers one said, "God bless us!" and the other responded with "Amen." The men expressed these wishes as though they had seen Macbeth with his "hangman's hands," that is, with his hands full of blood. Macbeth listened with fright. When the first man said, "God

bless us!" Macbeth wanted to reply, "Amen," but he was unable
to do so. Lady Macbeth tells him not to think about it. But
Macbeth wants to know why he could not say, "Amen." He
wants to know why the word stuck in his throat. She says that
if they keep thinking that way they will go mad. But Macbeth
continues in the same vein. He thought he heard a voice cry,
"Sleep no more! Macbeth does murder sleep. . . ." In recalling
what the voice had said Macbeth is reminded of the importance
in life of "innocent sleep." Sleep, Macbeth says in a series of
images, nightly soothes the spirit made sore by the difficulties
of daily life. After a short interruption by Lady Macbeth, to
which her husband seems to pay no attention, he continues to
talk of the voice he thought he heard. The voice continued to cry,
"Sleep no more! . . . Glamis hath murdered sleep, and therefore
Cawdor / Shall sleep no more, Macbeth shall sleep no more!"
Lady Macbeth is rattled by this and asks Macbeth who cried out
in that way. But she recovers her composure and tells Macbeth
that he makes himself weakspirited to think in this way; he must
get some water and wash away the blood from his hands which
would reveal his having done the murder. She now notices for
the first time the daggers he has brought with him from the scene
of the crime, and she tells him to return them and to smear the
faces of the grooms with blood. Macbeth refuses to return. It is
bad enough that he is afraid to think of his crime; he dares not
look at it again. His wife derides his weakness ("Infirm of
purpose!"), takes the daggers, tells him that sleeping and dead
people are like pictures feared only by children; if Duncan is
bleeding, she herself will smear the grooms' faces with blood.
And she goes to perform her task.

Macbeth is left alone. A knocking can be heard. Macbeth has
turned so many ordinary night noises into frightening ones that
he thinks the knocking is another ordinary night noise his
imagination has turned into a dangerous one. He looks at his
hands. They are so bloody, he thinks, that they are blinding him.
He wonders whether the ocean can wash his hands clean. They
cannot, he says; rather, his bloody hands will make all the seas
of the world red. Lady Macbeth re-enters and tells him that her

hands are also red, but she is ashamed to have a coward's heart ("a heart so white"). She hears the knocking, which is at the south gate. She tells her husband that they must go to their bedroom. "A little water clears us of this deed: / How easy is it then." That is, once they have washed their hands, how easy it will be not to feel guilty and to fool people into believing that they have not committed the deed. Macbeth apparently remains immobile, for his wife says "Your constancy / Hath left you unattended." That is, your firmness has deserted you. The knocking is heard once more, and she urges Macbeth to move so that he can appear as though he has just awakened. He finally exits showing his regret, "Wake Duncan with thy knocking: I would thou couldst!"

Critical analysis. Lady Macbeth has felt the need of wine to make her strong enough for the wickedness of the night. She hears an owl and likens it to the bell-man (or town crier) who, giving the "stern'st good-night," visited London prisoners on the night before execution. The owl and the bell-man, John Orrell notes, were conflated in *Blurt, Master Constable* (1602). Macbeth, she believes, is murdering Duncan; and she takes pleasure in the thoroughness with which the drugged possets are working upon Duncan's grooms. One might observe in passing that *wine, to which the plebeian grooms were unaccustomed, would have a stronger effect upon them*, according Elizabethan thinking, than upon Lady Macbeth. At l. 8 Macbeth calls without hysteria; and Lady Macbeth, not knowing whether it is the awaking grooms, shows a distinct preference, if something should go wrong, for being blamed for the deed itself rather than for attempting the deed. Although she says that she would have killed Duncan herself if it were not for his resemblance, when asleep, to her father, the text indicates that she resolves only to steel her husband for the deed. When she calls on the spirits to unsex her, she is identifying herself imaginatively with the deed. Her only physical part in the murder is the drugging and the smearing of the grooms. We are never sure that Macbeth will kill Duncan until he does it because there is always a chance that a sight of the intended victim will restore him to his senses. The deed is committed, we learn from V.i.35–36, shortly after two in the morning. Suspense collapses at once, but for Jacobean spectators there was still the suspenseful possibility that the remorseful Macbeth will repent.

Human blood and the sea. Macbeth, entering, tells of hearing Donalbain and Malcolm's awaking and praying. So we gather that the King's sons "feel for" his murder. *Macbeth's inability to pronounce the "Amen" should be interpreted as a sign of the assurance of his damnation in the theological sense.* When Lady Macbeth says, "These deeds must not be thought / After these ways," Kittredge comments, "in such a fashion as this (with an agonizing dwelling on every little detail, and perplexity as to what it means)." But surely she is telling Macbeth not to give heed to religious scruples. Macbeth recounts hearing a voice crying "Sleep no more"—a sign that his mind is beginning to break under the strain of the murder. He then delivers with his usual verbal felicity a short speech (ll. 33 ff.) on sleep that has, as Jean Robertson shows, a number of classical and Elizabethan parallels. The expression "great nature's second course," a phrase obscure to us, would appear to be a figure referring to the most substantial part of an Elizabethan dinner. Disgusted with Macbeth's being so "brain-sickly," Lady Macbeth grabs daggers and goes herself to place them by the grooms and smear the grooms with Duncan's blood. She is not sure if the old man has any flowing blood; but if he has, she will "gild the faces of the grooms withal, / For it must seem their guilt"—*a pun exhibiting her self-command or*, conceivably, *her repression of her guilt.* Macbeth, whose rhetorical strength grows in soliloquy, communes with himself on the impossibility of washing Duncan's blood from his hands: " . . . my hand will rather / The multitudinous seas incarnadine, / Making the green one red." The last line, Russell K. Alspach assures us, should be read, "Making the green—one red," a nuance that goes back to the actors Sheridan and Murphy. The passage is not so hyperbolical as has been thought if it is remembered that Renaissance people were accustomed to seeing analogies between the human body and the earth, specifically between human blood and the sea.

Lady Macbeth enters with bloody hands. She chides her husband for his white heart, meaning that in her view his behavior intimates that he is now totally lacking in virility, which she customarily identifies with the ability to perform bloody deeds of resolution without regard to their morality. *Repeated knocking, significantly at the south entrance (associated in this play with England and in general, with the east, a direction allied with moral goodness), means that the murder will shortly produce moral consequences.*

ACT II, SCENE iii

Plot summary. The scene is really a continuation of the previous one. The knocking at the gate heard by Macbeth and his wife is still heard after they leave the stage, and soon after the porter, whose job it is to open the gate, enters. His speech is in prose. "Here's a knocking, indeed!" he says. "If a man were porter of hell-gate, he should have old turning the key." That is, if a man were assigned the job of opening the gate of hell for the dead people who were sent there, he would have plenty to do ("should have old") turning the key. He hears the knocking again, and his remark about the porter of hell-gate apparently prompts him to play a game. He imagines himself to be the porter of hell-gate, and he thinks of types for whom he would be opening the gate and the reasons why these types would be coming to hell. The first is "a farmer, that hanged himself on the expectation of plenty. . . ." The farmer, the porter means, hanged himself because he had stored up grain originally expecting bad crops and high prices; but it now appeared as though the crops would be good and the prices would therefore be low; so, on the "expectation of plenty" he hangs himself. The next man is "an equivocator, that could swear in both scales against either scale; . . . yet could not equivocate to heaven. . . ." An equivocator is a man who purposely says something that has one meaning for most people hearing it but another meaning for himself. That is why he can swear on either side of the scale of justice against the other side. The third type is "an English tailor come hither for stealing out of a French hose...." The English tailor had copied what he thought was the current French style just as that had changed. Since Englishmen followed the French style, he thought the copying would make him popular. But he outsmarted himself. The porter hears the persistent knocking at the gate. "Never at quiet," he says. He is about to continue with another type when he remarks, "But this place is too cold for help. I'll devil-porter it no further: I had thought to have let in some of all professions, that go the primrose way to the everlasting bonfire." That is, he was going to show those in each profession who cheat and make it easy for themselves and therefore go to hell. He opens the gate for the men who have been knocking and *asks them for a tip* ("I pray you, remember the porter").

Macduff and Lennox are the men who have been knocking. Macduff asks whether the porter's sleeping late is a sign that he had gone late to bed. The porter answers that the people of the house had gone to bed at 3 A.M. ("the second cock") because they were up drinking. An exchange of shady dialogue about lechery and equivocation follows until Macbeth enters.

There follows some courteous greeting between him and the two thanes. It is Macduff's duty to wake the king, and he goes off to do so. Lennox talks about the stormy night that has just past. Among other things, chimneys were blown down, "strange screams of death" were heard as well as "lamentings . . . i' the air." Macbeth replies, "'Twas a rough night." Macduff then rushes out shouting the news of Duncan's murder: "Most sacreligious murder hath broke ope / The Lord's anointed temple...." Macbeth and Lennox go out to confirm Macduff's report. Macduff rings the alarm bell and wakes the house. Lady Macbeth and then Banquo enter. Hearing of Duncan's murder, Lady Macbeth cries, "What! in our house?" When Macbeth re-enters with Lennox, the former says that if he had died an hour before the accident of Duncan's murder he would have thought of his life as blessed. He goes on to say, "The wine of life is drawn, and the mere lees / Is left this vault to brag of." That is, the best part of life is over. Malcolm and Donalbain enter and discover what has happened, and Malcolm asks who has done the deed. Lennox replies that because the grooms were covered with blood it seems as though they had done it. Macbeth says that he is sorry he has killed the grooms. To Macduff's question as to why he did so, Macbeth replies that in the cross-current of violent emotions he felt upon seeing Duncan dead he had killed the attendants "to make's love [for Duncan] known." When Macbeth finishes telling his story about the killing of the grooms, Lady Macbeth faints (indicated by "Help me hence, ho!"). During the excitement brought on by Lady Macbeth's fainting Malcolm and Donalbain decide that in the currently dangerous situation they had better leave in a hurry. Lady Macbeth is carried out, and Banquo says that as soon as they are all properly dressed they will confer as to what to do. They all agree. Everyone but Malcolm and Donalbain exits. The latter decide that, in the situation as it stands, the false man easily shows false sorrow. Malcolm will go to England; Donalbain to Ireland. They will be safer if each goes a different way. Malcolm concludes by saying that, since there is no mercy left, there is good reason to steal oneself away.

Critical analysis. The Porter's soliloquy serves a variety of functions—dramatic irony, comic relief, foreshadowing, theme, the introduction of topical allusions, and a separation between the exeunt of the Macbeths and their re-entrance. As comic relief, the present scene is analogous to the grave-scene in *Hamlet* and to the representation of the clown with asps in *Antony and Cleopatra.* It would appear that the Porter is guarding a gate locking off one wing of the castle from another. The Porter fancies himself as playing the role of Satan's gatekeeper, who would of course be busier than the Porter himself: *porter* derives from L. "porta," gate. (One might well remember that during the Renaissance words of Latin and Greek origins were closer to their original meanings than the same words nowadays.) Someone has happily remarked, with reference to the

Porter's mental state, that his speech reflects "the sea-green clarity of the hang-over, not the crimson fantasies of the debauch." Curiously, the Porter bears some resemblance to Macbeth in that he has a low grade of poetic invention. *In Polanski's filmed version*, which at this point summons up a believable picture of medieval society with animals in the courtyard, men in dirty jerkins, and a sword dance, *the Porter urinates while delivering his speech*. Needless to say, the Porter ought to speak with a lower-class accent. With a number of allusions to the Gunpowder Plot of 1605, the speech may be presumed to have been electrifying to the chief intended victim, King James I.

Allusions to Jesuits. The Porter says, "Here's a farmer, that hang'd himself on th' expectation of plenty." H. L. Rogers thinks that this may be an allusion to Henry Garnet, the chief Jesuit of England, who was tried for complicity in the Gunpowder Plot, found guilty, and executed: one of Garnet's aliases was "Farmer." J. B. Harcourt thinks that the next speech should read, "Come in, Time," "for that relentless figure presides over the action of the play." "You'll sweat for't," in addition to the idea of sweating in Hell, carries with it, Harcourt believes, a sexual jest on *the sweating tub, the standard Elizabethan treatment of venereal disease*. "Faith, here's an equivocator, that could swear in both the scales against either scale, who committed treason enough for God's sake, yet could not equivocate to heaven." This remark is regarded as a clear allusion to Garnet and the Jesuits, who supposedly made ambiguous answers to questions and then swore to their truth. Frank L. Huntley, who has studied the background of the doctrine of equivocation (he has been corrected on a number of points by A. E. Malloch), points out that in *Macbeth* equivocation originates from the Devil, the arch-traitor, and that Macbeth, who has entertained treasonous thoughts before meeting the Witches, accepts the spoken half of their thoughts and acts on the other, unspoken half as completing the "truth." Such thinking involves two times: the present and the future, the latter belonging in the case of the Jesuits to God, in the case of the Macbeths to the Devil. Huntley presents an instance of Jesuitical equivocation from the "bloody question" in *The Treatise of Equivocation* by Henry Garnet, S. J.: "if brigands ask, 'Where is the Queen? We are sent to murder your sovereign,' you must equivocate by, '*Nescio [ut te dicam]*'—I know not *[to the end of telling you]*." *Scale* refers to "the exact balance between the two meanings of the ambiguous assertion."

Meanings of "tailor." "Faith, here's an English tailor come hither for stealing out of a French hose. Come in, tailor, here you may roast your goose." Tailors were proverbially thought to steal material. Since French hose (breeches) were tight-fitting and required little cloth, this kind of thievery would take skill. Rogers is of the opinion that there is an allusion here to an English tailor named Hugh Griffin, who was examined in late 1606 for a possible connection in the matter of Father Garnet's miraculous head of straw that was bothering authorities who feared the political consequences of Garnet's martyrdom, as Catholics conceived it. A very different interpretation, which may of course be held simultaneously, is Hilda Hulme's belief that *tailor* may be a euphemism for "penis," and that Gallic pox, *i.e.*, syphilis, is in view.

Associations with knocking. The Porter opens the gate with a request ("remember the porter") for a tip, and Macduff's insistent knocking is rewarded with a few light but dramatically important moments. J. W. Spargo observes that the knocking on the gate would not have been comic to the first audiences because it would have reminded the learned of Horace's line concerning the equality of death in kicking (Romans kicked doors) the doors of both rich and poor, and it would have summoned up for all ranks the rough knocking made by spade handles of citizens who entered houses to remove the corpses of those struck down by the plague. Glynne Wickham thinks the powerful knocking to be an overlay of the Harrowing of Hell scenes in certain English miracle (*i.e.*, mystery) plays. If so, Macduff suggests Christ knocking at the door of Hell to release the souls of patriarchs and prophets; and one with this memory would expect Macduff to be the avenger of Duncan's murder.

The Porter says to Macduff, ". . . drink, sir, is a great provoker of three things." It is difficult indeed to imagine this Scottish laird Macduff playing straight man to the Porter, "What three things does drink especially provoke?" The Porter punningly responds with application to drink as an "equivocator" who gives its user the "lie." " . . . though he [much drink] took up my legs sometime, yet I made a shift to cast him"—*here the Porter* employing language suggestive of uroscopy, *i.e.*, detection of illness by examination of urine, combined with the language of a purge or vomit, *grossly puts forward a thematic idea* in *Macbeth* that *evil will be expelled from the body politic*. Harcourt points out that the Porter's dealing with fornication and drunkenness—sins possessing a degree of human warmth—and his noting of the coldness of Macbeth's castle help to call our attention to Macbeth's monstrosity in evil. Frederic B. Tromly, however, thinks of *the Porter as a metaphor for Macbeth*: he points out that the Porter takes Macbeth's crime and translates it to "the familiar realm of diminished moral expectation." Both men lose themselves in "brainsickly" thoughts; both are reluctant to perform their offices; the Witches' equivocations are in effect like the Porter's drink. Tromly sees correspondences between Macbeth and the Porter in virtually every detail of the scene. On the other hand, M. J. B. Allen regards *the Porter as Macbeth's evil genius*: the drunk's tumescence is an analog of Macbeth's inability to beget children; Macbeth from this point on becomes spiritually degenerate; and the Porter, by letting in Macbeth's executioner, betrays Macbeth's soul to Hell.

Macbeth enters, and Macduff indicates that he has been commanded to waken the King. Macduff leaves for this purpose. Lennox and Macduff, we apprehend, have slept in a place separated by the gate from the King's wing, a point that absolves them from complicity in the murder, and one that makes it possible for them, whose quarters were in a more exposed part of the castle, to have heard the strange prodigies of the night. Prodigies announce or accompany the death of a great man also in *Julius Caesar*, II.ii.17–24.

Macbeth's low tolerance of suspense. Macduff bursts in with the horrendous report of regicide, set forth in terms combining language from Biblical verses like II Cor. 6, 16—"Ye are the temple of the living God" and I Sam. 24, 10, "the Lord's anointed." Showing that he cannot endure suspense, Macbeth leaves to murder the grooms, a crime not part (see II.ii.45–47) of the original plan. Macduff bawls out to awaken the sleepers, "Rise as at Doomsday and walk like white spirits to give the right setting to this horror." *The clang of the bell, as well as the earlier knocking on the gate, has been thought to symbolize Macbeth's agitation and convulsion in the murdering of Duncan.*

Lady Macbeth enters, Shakespeare here being wisely in defiance of an old acting version that required the Lady's absence from II.iii. She should be in the middle of the clamorous hall, *not* in her room, so that her self-possession might regard the nervous Macbeth and, if need be, take command. She does make a slip in her role as gentle hostess when she says, "What, in our house?" for which she is checked by Banquo, "Too cruel anywhere."

Macbeth re-enters, and by the eloquence of his lines (ll. 91–96) suggests that a politician is never more emotionally sincere than when commemorating a fallen rival. "Discovering" that Duncan's grooms have killed the King, Macbeth confesses that he has killed the grooms in an orgy of emotion and has not questioned them. *Macduff's response*, "Wherefore did you so?" *does not, one thinks, indicate either anger or suspicion but rather a desire to interrogate the grooms.* Macbeth vividly describes the stricken Duncan, "His silver skin lac'd with his golden blood." Duncan's blood differs from other blood—a pervasive image in the play—in that it is not thick and fearfully colored. W. A. Murray connects Duncan's "golden blood" with an alchemical agent capable, because of its perfections, of transmuting baser substances into something like itself.

Why Lady Macbeth faints. Lady Macbeth then faints, and a glance at the Variorum *Macbeth* is sufficient to gather that her motive has excited much discussion: is it genuine or histrionic? On the one side several considerations may be adduced. Her blunder about "What, in our house?" puts her under strain. She may be nervous about Macbeth's magniloquent prating upon something that a few minutes before he was afraid to look upon. She is quite unprepared for her husband's murder of the two grooms. She is constitutionally averse to bloodshed. She has not been able to relieve her mind with words. Madness and destruction seem to lie at the back of her mind (cf. II.ii.31). On the other hand, her fainting may be a feint to divert attention from the murder and to make herself appear innocent. Donalbain, in an aside "Our tears are not yet brew'd," suggests that the young princes may think the lamentation of the host and hostess to be synthetic. Malcolm perhaps means by ll. 139–40 that *we who are near in blood to the murdered King are nearer to being made bloody*, *i.e.*, murdered. Malcolm and Donalbain do not even trust Banquo or anyone else who is present: *one should note Malcolm's suspicion of Macduff in IV.iii.*

ACT II, SCENE iv

Plot summary. The scene occurs outside Macbeth's castle. Ross and an old man enter. The old man says that he can remember things for seventy years back, but he cannot remember a night as stormy as this has been. Ross replies by saying that the heavens are behaving as though they are troubled by "man's act," that is, last night's murder, and are threatening man. He goes on to say that, although the clock says that it is daytime, yet it is as dark as night. The old man answers, "'Tis unnatural, / Even like the deed that's done." And the old man and Ross talk of other unnatural events that have recently occurred, which fit with the last night's event and the present day's darkness. For example, Duncan's horses, previously tamed, turned wild and ate each other. Macduff now enters and tells the two who have been on stage the common belief concerning the murder. Malcolm and Donalbain, who have fled, hired the grooms to kill Duncan. He continues with the news that Macbeth has already been named king and has gone to be crowned at Scone, where Scottish kings are crowned. Duncan has been taken for burial. Ross asks Macduff whether he is going to the coronation at Scone, and Macduff replies, "No cousin; I'll to Fife." (Fife is Macduff's home; he is the Thane of Fife.) Ross says that he will go to Scone, and Macduff replies, "Well, may you see things well done there . . . / Lest our old robes sit easier than our new!" And each leaves on his own way.

Critical analysis. Between II.iii and II.iv the princes escape, the electors choose Macbeth as king, and Macbeth and his lady leave for Scone to be crowned. The chief purpose of this scene is to keep before us the connection between the material storms and the spiritual storms. The dramatic function of the nameless Old Man is to deliver *apocalyptic omens, the earthquake and eclipse reminding one of Christ's crucifixion and tending, therefore, to make Duncan a Christ-figure.* Another of the Old Man's prodigies is Duncan's horses eating each other: here we see *the most monstrous example of the pervasive horse-and-rider imagery of the play.* Horses were viewed in Elizabethan times as illustrations of unbridled violence: the *Homily against Wilful Rebellion*, for example, states that unmarried men when they revolt "pursue other men's wives and daughters . . . worse than any stallions or horses."

Macduff, entering, informs Ross and the Old Man of the "official theory" of the murder: the guilty grooms were bribed, suspicion says by Malcolm and Donalbain, to do the deed. Macduff apparently accepts the theory; but his answers are short, and he declines to attend the investiture of Macbeth. The crown goes to Macbeth, we apprehend, because Malcolm, the legal claimant, has repudiated the duty of claiming it. Macduff at ll. 36–37 fears that Macbeth's reign may not be so agreeable to the nobility as Duncan's. In the last lines of the scene the seerlike Old Man, speaking to Macduff and Ross, may harbor some suspicion of Macbeth.

ACT III, SCENE i

Plot summary. The scene takes place in the palace of the king of Scotland at Forres. As we learned in the last act, Macbeth is now king. Banquo enters and speaks a soliloquy. As though he is talking to Macbeth, he says, "Thou hast it now, King, Cawdor, Glamis, all / As the weird women promised. . . . " That is, you now have all the titles promised you by the Witches. And Banquo goes on to say that Macbeth attained the titles "most foully." But Banquo remembers the rest of the prophecy. No descendants of Macbeth would be kings; yet Banquo himself would be the forebear of a line of kings. If the prophecy for Macbeth came true, why should not the prophecy for Banquo come true and make him hopeful. But he sees Macbeth, Lady Macbeth and their party enter and he must be quiet.

Among the attendants of the king and queen are Lennox and Ross. Macbeth's first words refer to Banquo, "Here's our chief guest." Lady Macbeth adds that to forget Banquo is to have a "gap in our great feast." Macbeth formally announces the "solemn supper" they will hold tonight, and he formally invites Banquo. Banquo accepts the invitation. In the course of apparently casual conversation, Macbeth finds out from Banquo that Banquo and his son, Fleance, are going horseback riding and that they will not be back until after dark. During this conversation we also learn that Malcolm and Donalbain, whom Macbeth calls "our bloody cousins," are in England and Ireland. They do not confess "their cruel parricide," that is, the murder of their father, and they make up strange stories. Banquo leaves and Macbeth tells everyone to do as he wishes until the feast that evening. Macbeth commands a servant to bring in some men who are waiting for him. While he waits for the men, Macbeth is left alone on the stage, and he speaks a soliloquy.

"To be thus is nothing, but to be safely thus . . . ," says Macbeth. That is, to be king has no meaning unless one is securely a king.

Macbeth is afraid of Banquo. Banquo has the character of a king, which contains something to be afraid of: Banquo is daring, fearless, and wise enough to act safely. Macbeth is afraid of no one but Banquo, for Macbeth's angel ("My Genius") is always put down by Banquo. Banquo chastised the Witches when they first called Macbeth king and asked them to speak to him, Banquo. They told Banquo that he would be the forebear of "a line of kings" and upon Macbeth's head they placed "a fruitless crown, / And put a barren sceptre in my gripe. . . ." That is, since Macbeth would be childless no descendants of his would be kings. If this is so, Macbeth has given up his immortal soul ("eternal jewel") to the devil ("the common enemy of man") only to make kings of Banquo's descendants. Rather than allow this to be the case, Macbeth challenges fate. But he is interrupted in his thoughts by the entrance of the servant bringing his two visitors.

The servant enters with the two men whom the stage directions call Murderers. In the course of Macbeth's conversation with them we learn that they have had a previous interview with him. He told them in that interview that where they had thought it was Macbeth who had deceived them with false promises, it was in actuality Banquo. Macbeth then goes on to the point of the current meeting. He tries to persuade them that if they are men, they will not take their betrayal lying down. The First Murderer has answered only very briefly until this point. Now he says in a speech of three lines that his luck has been so bad that he is desperate and does not care what he does. The Second Murderer in a speech equally long agrees with the First. Macbeth tells them that Banquo is also Macbeth's enemy. Although he could kill Banquo with "bare-faced power," yet he dare not do it because of the mutual friends that he and Banquo have, whose love he is afraid to lose. Therefore, he asks the two men to take care of his business privately. They give their consent. Macbeth will advise them as to the place. And they must kill Fleance also, for Fleance's death is as important to Macbeth as Banquo's. The Murderers agree and leave. Macbeth concludes with "Banquo, thy soul's flight, / If it find Heaven, must find it out tonight."

Critical analysis. The unclear time lapse between Acts II and III permits us only to gather that Macbeth has been crowned for some time. Banquo in soliloquy shows awareness that Macbeth may have engineered his becoming king; but although Banquo is, by analogy with Macbeth's rise, inclined to place some credence in the Witches' prophecies, he is not inclined to criminal action himself, partly because he does not know whether his immediate or his remote descendants will become kings. He does not feel a need to hide himself, as Macduff does, from Macbeth's administration partly because, unlike Macduff, he has no great estate or fief. *It is not customary to decline support to an able politician who has perhaps used unfair tactics in putting down the opposition and who now promises a fair administration!* Bradley opines that Banquo is in this speech yielding to evil, but Kirschbaum with more cogency argues that "But hush, no more" is not said to dismiss "cursed thoughts," but merely to register Banquo's *hearing the sennet* announcing the entrance of the King and Queen.

Macbeth, entering, shows his graciousness to Banquo by employing, in l. 15, *the personal "I" rather than the royal "we" in issuing a command* for Banquo to appear at a "solemn supper" this evening. Banquo in response mentions "a most indissoluble tie" between Macbeth and himself, alluding to the prophecies of the Witches and his suspicions of Macbeth's making himself king, neither of which Banquo seems ever to have communicated to anyone else. Macbeth shows much interest in the details of Banquo's riding forth with Fleance because he wants to murder them both. Curiously, Banquo exhibits no suspicion about this line of inquiry. It would be a mistake, should Fleance be onstage, for the actor playing Macbeth to fondle him in a catlike manner at l. 35, for Macbeth is not a sadist. He fears Banquo because of what Macbeth knows of Banquo's character and of the prophecy; and he wants Banquo out of the way at once, rather than later, because at the council of state indicated in ll. 32–34 he will have to confront Banquo publicly on what "our bloody cousins" are putting forth in the way of "strange invention."

A great soliloquy and its symbolism. In the great soliloquy that follows, Macbeth fears not so much Banquo the man as Banquo the symbol, as Kirschbaum points out, of virtues that Macbeth wants but cannot have. In saying " . . . under him, / My Genius is rebuk'd," Macbeth is in effect saying, "My genius of intemperate ambition for the crown rebuked by his steadfast loyalty even in the face of provocation." Although Shakespeare is sometimes credited with causing characters who speak in soliloquy to tell therein the straight truth, *it is not true* that Banquo "chid the sisters / When first they put the name of king upon me, / And bade them to speak to him"; for Banquo spoke to them fairly and dispassionately. Macbeth reports (ll. 60–63) the Witches as prophesying that he would be childless; the fact of the matter is that they did not say this. The prospect of kingship must seem absolutely good to Macbeth when it is first offered. By III.i Macbeth realizes that he has gained nothing by the murder of Duncan; and now the prophecy of his lack of progeny is brought in as it were by stealth. In l. 69 "seeds" rather than "seed" should be used because Shakespeare wrote it that way, and this emendation that Alexander Pope made does not so well convey the multiplication of Banquo's issue. Macbeth thinks that he has made a bad bargain—he has entered the ranks of the damned for no better reason than to make Banquo's posterity kings. Ll. 70–71 mean "Let fate fight as my champion until I am killed," not as Dr. Johnson thought, "let fate enter the lists against me."

Motivating the Murderers. The two Murderers enter: they are Scottish gentlemen, maddened by despair, previously enemies of Macbeth but now convinced that Banquo has wronged them; by contrast Lady Macduff's Murderers are common cutthroats. Macbeth endeavors to steel the murderers for the killing of Banquo by asking them whether they are so full of Christian grace that they can pray for their wrongdoers. Macbeth's "dog" speech, ll. 91 ff., exhibits moral confusion from the point of view of Renaissance orthodoxy because it confuses dogs and men; and, one might add, it shows Macbeth not far removed from his wife's conception of manhood. Both Murderers are utterly reckless, but Macbeth is willing to use them to make it appear that Banquo's death is the result of a feud. Macbeth says, honestly enough, that he must not sweep Banquo into death in an open manner lest doing so should aggrieve certain mutual friends. The Murderers appear resolved although *we learn later that they are reluctant*: Macbeth sends a Third Murderer in III.iii. One might think of ending this scene with the following business: "At the close of Macbeth's colloquy with the villains whom he employs to murder Banquo, those wretches try, with fawning servility, to seize the hem of his regal robe, and thereupon he repulses them with a deportment of imperial disdain and a momentary shudder." But this interpolated action would reduce these decayed gentlemen to the level of hired thugs.

ACT III, SCENE ii

Plot summary. We are still in the king's castle at Forres. Lady Macbeth enters with a servant. Lady Macbeth asks the servant whether Banquo has as yet left the court, that is, has he yet gone riding. The servant replies that he has but that he will be back in the evening. The mistress sends her servant for Macbeth, and Lady Macbeth is left alone. She has a short speech before Macbeth enters. "Naught's had, all's spent / Where our desire is got without content . . . ," she says. That is, when one has attained one's goal without mental ease and satisfaction, all the effort used to attain the goal has been put forth for nothing. She continues by saying that it is safer to be the murdered person ("that which we destroy") than to be the murderer living in uncertain happiness ("dwell in doubtful joy").

Macbeth enters, and his wife berates him. Why, she asks, does he isolate himself with his unhappy thoughts? Those thoughts about the dead should have died with them. Things that cannot be helped should not be thought about. "What's done is done." Macbeth replies that they have slashed the snake in two; they have not killed it; the snake will re-form into a whole. Macbeth uses figurative language to say that in killing Duncan and his two grooms Macbeth and his wife have not completely eliminated their danger; because the danger has not been completely eliminated, it will again be as great as once it was. He goes on to tell Lady Macbeth that he will let the entire universe disintegrate before he and his wife "will eat our meal in fear, and sleep / In the affliction of these terrible dreams, / That shake us nightly." It is better, he says, to be with the dead whom they have killed to gain peace (for the ambitions) than to be in constant mental anguish. Duncan is dead, and nothing in this life can hurt him any more. Lady Macbeth tells her husband to take it easy and to be happy at the feast that evening. He says that he will be happy and that she should be happy too. She ought to pay special attention to Banquo: while they are unsafe, their faces must mask their hearts. "You must leave this," says Lady Macbeth. "O! full of scorpions is my mind, dear wife!" answers her husband. That is, my mind is full of evil thoughts. Macbeth adds, "Thou know'st that Banquo, and his Fleance, lives." She replies that they do not live forever. "There's comfort yet," says her husband. He tells her that Banquo and Fleance are vulnerable. He adds that before night a dreadful deed shall be done. "What's to be done?" she asks. "Be innocent of the knowledge, dearest chuck, / Till thou applaud the deed." That is, you do not have to know about the deed, darling, until it is over, at which time you can praise me for it. Macbeth now makes an invocation to night. He asks night to come and to blindfold the eye of day, which is full of pity; and night, he continues, with its "bloody and invisible hand," will then destroy "that great bond / Which keeps me pale!" (the lives of Banquo and Fleance). Apparently, night once more answers Macbeth's command, for he now says, "Light thickens," and he goes on to describe the onset of night, which again reflects the state of his mind: " . . . night's black agents to their preys do rouse." Lady Macbeth evidently gazes at her husband in astonishment, for he remarks to her, "thou marvell'st at my words. . . ." He goes on to observe that things begun badly improve themselves by continued evil. "So, pr'ythee, go with me," says he as they exeunt.

Critical analysis. In this scene Macbeth is brooding about Banquo's still being alive. Lady Macbeth, in language equating Banquo's continued life with unsatisfying sexual performance, shares her husband's fear. Macbeth, entering, observes that although his enemies have been wounded, there is still life and menace in them. Amneus argues that this passage strongly suggests, and Forman's report of the Globe performance confirms, that Banquo's murder has already taken place: the Folio text has been cut. (The word should be "scotched" the snake, not "scorched" it.) He expects "Malice domestic" from Banquo and Macduff, "foreign levy" from Malcolm in England and Donalbain in Ireland. Lady Macbeth advises him to take his mind off his sleeplessness and Duncan's sleeping in his grave; he should prepare, she says, for the feast tonight. He replies, "O, full of scorpions is my mind, dear wife!" *The scorpion image may be derived from the traditional inconography that made the scorpion a symbol of Judas, a view that enriches analogies with the betrayal of Christ and Macbeth's murder of Duncan.* However, Dennis Biggins is disposed to *regard the scorpion* on the basis of medieval and Renaissance thought *as a secular emblem of flattering treachery*: as such, the word brings to focus the theme of false appearances. *Scorpions were in Shakespeare's time thought to be serpents*, and Macbeth is adjured by his wife in I.v to be the serpent under the innocent flower. There is notable irony in Macbeth's playing the snake and acting the scorpion *vis-à-vis* Duncan and then finding serpents under every innocent flower. Macbeth continues, "Thou know'st that Banquo, and his Fleance, lives." Lady Macbeth replies, "But in them nature's copy's not eterne." *The meaning of "nature's copy" has occasioned much discussion.* Matti Rissanen points out that there are two chief interpretations: *copy* in the sense of "copyhold," thus linking this metaphor with the idea (cf. III.ii.49; IV.i.99) that man holds his life from nature until death; *copy* in the sense of the human body as "a thing to be copied" or "the result of imitation." Recent editors of *Macbeth* tend to accept the second interpretation as primary. Macbeth responds, "There's comfort yet," in which *"There's"* should be emphasized. Macbeth's last speech sounds consciously literary and melodramatic as if, speaking a private incantation, he is trying to build his confidence. One may wonder why Macbeth does not here disclose to Lady Macbeth his plot against Banquo. There is no clear answer. He may wish to shield his wife from further guilt, or he may wish to avoid her further chiding. The former possibility, since he has grown bolder since the murder of Duncan, seems stronger. At any rate, Lady Macbeth knows at the end of the scene that Banquo and Fleance are to be killed.

ACT III, SCENE iii

Plot summary. The scene occurs in a park near the palace. Three Murderers enter. Two of them we know; they had the interview with Macbeth in the first scene of this act. The third one is known neither to us nor to the first two Murderers. The First Murderer asks, "But who did bid thee join us?" The First Murderer is apparently suspicious of the Third. The latter says that Macbeth told him to come. The Second Murderer says, "He needs not our mistrust. . . ." That is, we need not mistrust him. The reason why they need not distrust the Third Murderer, he says, is that the Third Murderer gives them all the directions Macbeth had promised they would receive. The First Murderer agrees and then describes the coming of night in lovely language. When he ends, the Third Murderer hears their vicitms. Banquo enters with Fleance, who is carrying a torch. Banquo says, "It will rain tonight." The First Murderer responds with "Let it come down." The First Murderer apparently then puts out the torch being carried by Fleance. The Murderers attack Banquo, who cries, "O, treachery! Fly, good Fleance, fly, fly, fly!" He dies, and Fleance escapes. The Third Murderer asks who put out the light. The First Murderer returns with the question, "Was't not the way?" That is, was not that the arrangement. They realize that Fleance has escaped, and the Second Murderer says, "We have lost / Best half of our affair." The First Murderer says that they ought to report to Macbeth, and they exeunt.

Critical analysis. Macbeth wishes to murder Banquo, his chief counselor, because Banquo stands ready through his children to take the throne. He does not himself murder Banquo for the apparent reason that if others do it, he feels that he will not be haunted by guilty thoughts: Macbeth says later to Banquo's Ghost, "Thou canst not say I did it" (III.iv.49). The Third Murderer is sent to give final orders to the other two assassins in accordance with Macbeth's promise (III.i.127 ff.); so the Third Murderer's appearance has been prepared for. We gather that the Third Murderer has Macbeth's confidence because he does not require briefing. As the Variorum edition testifies, *there has been discussion*, pro and con, *about the possibility that Macbeth is the Third Murderer. This view is incorrect for at least three reasons.* The interview between Macbeth and the First Murderer in III.iv.13 ff. would then become useless. This view transforms down-at-the-heels gentlemen-murderers into hireling assassins. If this view is held, as George W. Williams has shown, it violates *"The Law of Re-entry," i.e.*, Shakespeare's habitual adherence in plays at and before this time to the rule that a character who exits in the last line of a scene does not immediately re-enter at the first line of the following scene.

Cooling the hot horses. The First Murderer in ll. 5–8 gives a poetic chronological indication: he can do this because he has no "character" at all, *i.e.*, he is a personified set of functions. Banquo tells us, "It will rain tonight," intimating that the night is cloudy, ripe for murder, and that it therefore suits the mood of the Murderers. Act III, Scene iii suggests, according to Joan Blythe, that Banquo and Fleance are walking their horses the last mile through the park to the palace presumably to cool the hot beasts. When they are beset by the Murderers, who are on foot, Banquo cries to Fleance to "fly," meaning that Fleance is to remount and escape.

Bradley on Banquo. Banquo is killed onstage, one surmises, partly for the reason that the audience is thus prepared for his Ghost at the banquet. If his death atones for anything it is for the ambitious curiosity to know what the future has in store for him, for he thus incurs the jealousy of Macbeth. Bradley remarks, "When next we see him [Banquo], on the last day of his life, we find that he has yielded to evil. The Witches and his own ambition have conquered him. He alone of the lords knew the of prophecies, but he has said nothing of them. He has acquiesced in Macbeth's accession, and in the official theory that Duncan's sons had suborned the chamberlains to murder him. Doubtless, unlike Macduff, he was present at Scone to see the new king invested." But there is no hint that Banquo will play "most foully" to make the prophecy come true. One may think that Banquo is necessary for dramatic contrast, as a foil to Macbeth. After all, Macbeth is king, and subjects are to be loyal. Furthermore—the point is crucial—Banquo has no real evidence: it is not prudent to accuse any man, still less a king, of murder unless one has solid evidence. Fleance, in escaping, underscores the truth of the Witches' prophecy to Banquo.

ACT III, SCENE iv

Plot summary. This scene takes place in a room of the palace set for a banquet. Macbeth, Lady Macbeth, Ross, Lennox, other lords, and attendants enter. Macbeth says, "You know your own degrees, sit down. . . ." He tells them, in effect, that since they know their proper ranks, they can seat themselves according to rank without the formality of Macbeth's having to place them. After being thanked Macbeth goes on to say that he himself will mingle with the guests while the hostess (Lady Macbeth) remains on the throne. As the formalities of welcome continue, the First Murderer appears at the door. Macbeth continues talking but meanwhile making his way to the door. Presumably, the guests cannot see the First Murderer. Macbeth says to him, "There's blood upon thy face." The First Murderer replies that it is Banquo's blood. To this Macbeth says that he prefers Banquo's blood on the Murderer's skin than inside Banquo's body. The First Murderer assures Macbeth that Banquo is dead. Macbeth asks whether Fleance is also dead. The Murderer replies that Fleance has escaped. "Then comes my fit again: I had else been perfect . . . ," says Macbeth. That is, because Fleance has escaped, I am once more in a fit of fear; if he had not escaped, I would now be healthy. He continues in the same vein in a series of images, which are climaxed by "But now, I am cabin'd, cribb'd, confin'd bound / To saucy doubts and fears." He means that he is not to act normally at ease but subject to doubts and fears. "But Banquo's safe?" he adds. That is, is Banquo safely dead? The Murderer assures him that Banquo is "safe in a ditch . . . / With twenty trenched [cut] gashes on his head. . . ." Macbeth thanks the Murderer. Then in a metaphor in which Banquo and Fleance are compared to a grown serpent and the child serpent ("the worm") Macbeth says in effect that, although Banquo is dead, Fleance, who has escaped but offers no threat now, will one day present a threat. Macbeth tells the Murderer to leave, that they will have another interview tomorrow. The Murderer exits.

Lady Macbeth now calls to her husband, who has been absenting himself from the table. She tells him that the feast without Macbeth's ceremony of good cheer is like a feast not given. Macbeth becomes aware of his surroundings and begins to act hearty. Lennox asks Macbeth to sit at the table. Macbeth says that all of the men of distinction of the country would be here now if Banquo were present. And Banquo's absence, Macbeth tells his listeners, is due to Banquo's unkindness rather than to accident. While Macbeth has been speaking, Banquo's ghost enters. Now Ross asks Macbeth to be seated at the table. As Macbeth approaches the empty place at the table, the place reserved for him, he sees *his* place occupied by Banquo's ghost.

"The table is full," says Macbeth. The others cannot see the ghost. They tell Macbeth that there is a place for him. "Where?" asks Macbeth. "Here, my good lord," replies Lennox, who then asks Macbeth what is troubling him. Macbeth shouts at his guests, "Which of you have done this?" That is, who has killed Banquo? The guests do not know what Macbeth is talking about. Macbeth now shouts at the ghost, "Thou canst not say, I did it [the murder]; never shake / Thy gory locks at me." Ross tells the other lords to leave; Macbeth, he says, is not well. Lady Macbeth, however, intervenes. She tells the lords to sit. She says that Macbeth has had momentary fits since his youth and any attention paid to them extends the fit. She then whispers to Macbeth, "Are you a man?" He says that he is a bold man, for he dares "look on that / Which might appal the devil." Lady Macbeth pours contempt on her husband. He insistently points at the ghost, "Behold! look! . . . ." He then becomes desperate: "Why what care I?" And he challenges the ghost to speak.

The ghost disappears. Lady Macbeth continues to berate him, "What! quite unmann'd in folly?" Macbeth insists that, as he is alive, he saw him. We know of course that it is Banquo; Lady Macbeth, since she does not see the ghost, cannot be certain whom Macbeth sees. Whoever it is, she must set things in order again. "Fie! for shame!" she tells him. Macbeth says that in former times, when a man was murdered, he would stay dead; "but now, they rise again, / With twenty mortal murders on their crowns [heads], / And push us from our stools." Apparently the ghost of Banquo has the "twenty trenched gashes on its head" about which the First Murderer told Macbeth. The ghost, then, is all cut and bloody. Seeing that Macbeth is coming to himself again, Lady Macbeth says, "My worthy lord, / Your noble friends do lack you." That is, the guests miss him. Macbeth replies, "I do forget." He goes on to give for himself the same excuse Lady Macbeth had previously given for him, that he has a strange illness which, when it shows itself, does not surprise people who know him. He now offers a toast to everyone at the table, "And to our dear friend Banquo, whom we miss; / Would he were here!" At this point the ghost of Banquo reappears.

Macbeth sees it and shouts for it to leave his sight. He says, in effect, that since the ghost is only a ghost it ought to let itself be buried. Lady Macbeth tries to smooth things over again. She repeats that Macbeth's peculiar behavior is not extraordinary. "Only it spoils the pleasure of the time." Macbeth continues speaking to the ghost. He dares do anything a man would do: let the ghost appear in any form but that in which it now appears; let it appear in the form of a bear or a tiger or even the live Banquo, and Macbeth would fight with him. "Unreal mockery, hence!" That is, get away, you parody of reality. The ghost disappears. Since it has done so, Macbeth says, he is "a man again." He turns to his guests and tells them to sit still. Lady Macbeth says that he has destroyed everyone's good time. Macbeth, who thinks that the guests have also seen the ghost, cannot understand how they could have looked at such a sight without fear. Ross asks him what he has seen. Lady Macbeth intervenes and requests the lords not to speak; questions will make Macbeth only worse. "At once, good night": she says to them, "Stand not upon the order of your going, / But go at once." And all the lords leave.

Macbeth and Lady Macbeth are left alone. Macbeth says that no matter how secretly done, murder will out. He asks his wife the time, and she tells him that it is almost dawn. He now asks her what she thinks of Macduff's refusal to present himself at Macbeth's command. To her question as to whether he had sent for Macduff, Macbeth replies, "I hear it by the way ... / There's not a one of them, but in his house / I keep a servant fee'd." He goes on to tell her that he is going to see the Witches the next day. Then he says, "For mine own good, / All causes shall give way. . . ." He feels that he is so deep in blood "returning were as tedious as go o'er." He has strange things in his mind, he continues, which must be accomplished before they are thought about. Lady Macbeth tells him that he lacks what everyone has, sleep. "Come we'll to sleep," he says. His peculiar self-punishment, he goes on, is the fright that comes from first doing an evil deed. Evil has not yet become customary for them. "We are but young in deed," he says as the scene ends.

Critical analysis. The banquet scene presents *Macbeth* in microcosm because it *exhibits in Macbeth's mind and in Scottish society the movement from order to chaos* and because Macbeth comes here to a realization that there is a world over which he possesses no control, the world from which the dead return to "push us from our stools." J. P. Dyson divides it into *five parts or "movements"*: from the opening to the appearance of the First Murderer, wherein Macbeth's intentions of order are prominent; the conversation with the Murderer; the appearance of Banquo's Ghost, which is the turning point; the chaotic aftermath of the feast; and Macbeth's awareness of the wasteland of his existence.

Macbeth prepares a banquet for his nobles because he wishes not merely to be king but to have the hearts of his people. Lady Macbeth is seated in a chair of state or on a dais under a canopy. Macbeth is to sit at the head of the table because he is king and the nobles are commanded to sit in strict hierarchical order, and also because he wishes to go to the door easily. Since Banquo is not present, his seat has been removed to relieve awkwardness and to defer to the superstition against uneven numbers.

Macbeth then parleys with the First Murderer, whom he appropriately "thou's," and learns with joy that Banquo is dead and with fear that Fleance has escaped. Lady Macbeth recalls him to the feast.

Is it an objective ghost? At this point the Ghost of Banquo appears—so the stage direction in the First Folio has it—and sits in Macbeth's place. *There has been much debate about the objectivity of the Ghost.* The view taken here is that *for many reasons*—cited by E. E. Stoll and others—*the Ghost is to be viewed as a visual reality, not a hallucination of Macbeth's.* At sighting it Macbeth changes suddenly and totally from composure to frenzy. Macbeth and the Ghost are mutually hostile. Macbeth defies the Ghost. The Ghost is persistently vindictive, being sent to "religiously punish Macbeth." Macbeth brushed aside the appearance of the dagger, but he does not think of brushing aside the Ghost. At IV.i.112 he believes the Ghost to have been a visual reality. *The spectre appears before Macbeth discerns it*, and it is given stage directions. The fact that the Ghost declines to speak is not weighty because its purpose is to be inscrutably menacing, and Stoll cites *other instances in Elizabethan drama of silent and supposedly objective ghosts*. If one argues that the Ghost is subjective because the dagger and the voice, which Macbeth declares to be figments of the mind, have brought him to the point where he believes the Ghost to be real, why is he free from hallucinations after this point? One would expect him to commingle fact and fancy all the more. To be sure, Lady Macbeth and the guests do not see it; but *the nature of ghosts permitted a sighting to one observer and denied this to others* (cf. *Hamlet*, III.iv.101 ff.), and one might add that the guests are not in the position of the audience. *The Ghost sits in Macbeth's seat because Banquo's issue will take over the siege royal.*

In the Kurosawa filmed version Macbeth suddenly draws his sword upon the Ghost, the contrast between ceremony and irrational spontaneity becoming, as Michael Mullin says, "a dramatic metaphor for Macbeth's conflict between duty and ambition."

Macbeth cries, "Which of you have done this?" meaning "Which of you has killed Banquo?" *not* "Which of you has placed this corpse in my chair?" Lady Macbeth learns from this what is bothering her husband. The "gory locks" of Banquo's Ghost, a characteristic shared by his posterity (IV.i.113), suggest, as Blissett points, the virility and procreative quality of the line. At this point Lady Macbeth tries to quiet the shaken assembly, using "frightful smiles, overacted attention, and fitful graciousness" to divert notice from her husband.

The Lady now decides her husband needs disciplining, being "brainsickly" again. Accordingly ll. 57–83 are not meant to be heard by the banqueters. She chastises him again as one wanting manliness. Macbeth replies that he is bold enough to look on what might "appal" the Devil, meaning, according to Biggins, make the black Devil turn to white with fear.

Some traditional business. Macbeth becomes calm again, the Ghost having exited. In an access of hubris he toasts Banquo again, the Ghost having reappeared. Macbeth is here, as G. R. Elliott remarks, doing what politicians often do—he is expressing mock regard for a rival politician whom he has long wished to dispatch or have dispatched. More philosophically, he supposes that by the exertion of personal force he can impose his own order on the vicissitudes of existence. The traditional business here, which goes all the way back to a line in Beaumont's *The Knight of the Burning Pestle* that seems to reflect the way the play was acted, is Macbeth's dropping his cup. The second appearance of the Ghost is not anticlimactic, for this glassy-eyed creature has grown desperate to match Macbeth's growing boldness. It does not prophesy Macbeth's death because Macbeth dies not at the hands of Fleance but in combat with Macduff. The king chides the Ghost for not being a man, "Unreal mock'ry, hence!" meaning not that the Ghost is subjective but that as a shade it lacks substance. The banquet is broken up even to the point of the guests leaving, at Lady Macbeth's command, without regard to "degree."

Macbeth's conscience speaks, editors generally believe, to the effect that the murderer will be identified by means of the *auspicium*, divination of augurs by means of birds. This theory, according to Schanzer, fails to meet two difficulties: divination of murderers by means of birds has not been known anywhere; the birds mentioned here—magpies, choughs, rooks—have never been regarded as "auspicious." The probable meaning is that any ordinary bird might be endowed by the gods with the power of speech for the purpose of disclosing the identity of a murderer (in Chaucer's "Manciple's Tale" a crow reveals adultery), and then *understood relations* means simply "reports which could be understood."

Two Biblical allusions. Macbeth then turns his thoughts to

Macduff, who has not been present at the banquet, who has avoided attending the coronation (II.iv.36), remaining on his Fifeshire estate, but who has not positively refused a royal command. Macbeth gets wind of Macduff's intentions from a spy. The king tells his lady, "Returning were as tedious as go o'er." Here "returning" has the Old Testament sense (see Isa. 30, 15) of going back to the Lord and His way—the line should remind us that Macbeth still has the possibility of repenting although modern critics think of him as being "determined" to go on in bloodshed. Macbeth suggests that he will indulge an orgy of bloodshed, but his terms are so general that suspense is not completely removed.

The banquet scene loosely parallels Belshazzar's feast in that it is intended to signal an iniquitous success; it exhibits a supernatural omen presaging doom, and the doom itself. The scene fascinates partly because it moves on several levels. It marks the ending of Lady Macbeth's part of the action.

ACT III, SCENE v

Plot summary. The point of this scene seems to be that the Witches will make Macbeth feel secure, and his sense of security will lead him to destruction.

This scene and part of Act IV, Scene 1, permit the Witches to sing songs, which undoubtedly heightened the interest the Witches held for the audience. These songs are from a play, *The Witch*, by Shakespeare's contemporary, Thomas Middleton. Because the company used the songs from Middleton's play, some critics think that Middleton also wrote the insertions for this play. However, a number of scholars who know Middleton's work well are inclined to think otherwise.

Critical analysis. This scene serves by means of fantasy to provide relief from the harrowing banquet just as the Porter does with coarse humor after the murder. The author accounts for

Hecate's absence during the preceding part of the play by having her berate the Witches (ll. 2 ff.) for failing to call her in their dealings with Macbeth. Hecate's appearance, however, has been to some extent prepared for by Macbeth's imagination (II.i.52; III.ii.41); but the Hecate of III.v is more fairylike than we should expect. It has been wrongly suggested that ll. 2–13 reach "a climax of unfitness" in the allegation that Macbeth is pretending to be in love with the Witches: l. 13—"Loves for his own ends, not for you"—means that Macbeth is a lover of his own worldly success rather than of diabolism per se. Hecate says that Macbeth is but "a wayward son," meaning that he is not a true disciple of a demon-worshipping sect. He never goes to "the pit of Acheron" (l. 15), as Hecate says that he will do. Hecate in truth has only a tenuous connection with the Witches of the play. She leaves the scene, we gather, by a machine that lifts her into the "heavens" (ll. 34–35), an area above the balcony of the theater.

The song "Come away! Come away! / Hecate, Hecate, come away" is credited to Thomas Middleton inasmuch as it appears in his play titled *The Witch*. But Nosworthy points out that Middleton's Hecate is coarse, brusque, and colloquial, speaking mainly in blank verse, occasionally in irregular verse, and never in octosyllabic couplets. J. O. Wood believes that the literary quality of the scene rises above Middleton's known powers.

Wood has suggested that "profound" in "There hangs a vap'rous drop profound, / I'll catch it ere it come to ground" may be a truncated participle deriving from L. *profundere*, "to pour forth," rather than from L. *profundus*, "deep." When Hecate next appears, nothing is said of the "vap'rous drop."

ACT III, SCENE vi

Plot summary. Most editors locate this scene in the king's palace at Forres. In the original edition of the play it is unlocated, and some critics believe that this conversation could not occur in the king's palace filled with spies. *On the bare Elizabethan stage probably no one would have thought about where the scene takes place; only important was the fact that the scene developed the play's plot, atmosphere and idea.* The surface reality did not matter: the scene obviously occurs somewhere in Scotland, and we learn something about Macbeth and something about Scotland.

Lennox and an unnamed lord enter. Apparently, they are either in the midst of a conversation or they have previously discussed matters. For Lennox says that in his "former speeches" he has said what the lord had been thinking. Lennox then becomes obviously ironic. Macbeth pitied Duncan, and Duncan died. Banquo stayed out too late; it is possible to say that Fleance killed him because Fleance ran away. One must also think how terrible it was for Malcolm and Donalbain to kill their father. This made Macbeth so very unhappy that in religious anger he killed the murderers. He was wise to do it, too, for it would have made anyone angry to hear them deny the deed. Lennox thinks, therefore, that Macbeth has managed things well. And he also believes that if Malcolm, Donalbain, and Fleance were in Scotland, they should know what it is to kill a father. Lennox now changes the subject. He has heard that Macduff is not in the king's good graces because he has spoken "broad words," that is, Macduff has spoken too obviously—of course, too obviously against the king; and because he did not appear at the "tyrant's feast" (Macbeth's banquet). He wishes to know whether the lord can tell him where Macduff is.

The lord replies that "The son of Duncan, / From whom this tyrant holds the due of birth, / Lives in the English court. . . ." The lord must be talking about Malcolm, because we know that Malcolm said that he was going to England; and because we know that with Duncan's death, Malcolm should be on the throne. The lord then says that Malcolm lives at the English court of "the most pious Edward" (Edward the Confessor) who treats Malcolm very well. Macduff has gone there to ask Edward to encourage Siward, the Earl of Northumberland, to help Malcolm in an undertaking to overthrow Macbeth. This undertaking (if successful) would once more "Give to our tables meat, sleep to our nights, / Free from our feasts and banquets bloody knives . . . ." The report of all this has prompted Macbeth's sending for Macduff. Macbeth sent for him, continues the lord, but Macduff replied in a definite negative. When Macduff thus answered the messenger looked threateningly at him. Lennox says that Macduff should be cautious enough to retain a distance. He hopes that Macduff does well in England so that "a swift blessing / May soon return to this our suffering country / Under a hand accursed."

Critical analysis. Between III.iv and III.vi Macbeth summons Macduff; Macduff flees to England; and the Scottish nobles become suspicious of Macbeth. Lennox ironically argues that Malcolm and Donalbain engineered their father's murder. What is the proof? Their flight. Fleance has killed Banquo. The proof? His flight. Lennox should know whereof he speaks with regard to the slaughter of the drunken grooms, for he was an eyewitness. The English king to whom Malcolm has fled is known to history as Edward the Confessor, who reigned before the Norman Conquest.

An interesting question posed by the flight of Macduff to England is *how Lennox and the anonymous lord in III.vi come by their knowledge of Macduff's whereabouts* when Macbeth learns of this matter only after the cauldron scene (IV.i). The somewhat unsatisfying answer is that these persons know more than their king does. One ought to bear ll. 39–43 in mind when we later come to the murder of Lady Macduff: the Lady does not know the consequences of Macduff's failure to attend the royal court; she thinks that her husband is animated by irrational fear. If we suppose that Lady Macduff is merely given to complaining we miss much of the dramatic quality of IV.ii.

ACT IV, SCENE i

Plot summary. The scene occurs in a cavern in the middle of which is a boiling cauldron. The Three Witches enter. As they speak a charm, with which they hope to secure Macbeth, they throw into their boiling pot such parts of repulsive animals as the eye of a newt, the wool of a bat, and a lizard's leg. The refrain of their charm is "Double, double toil and trouble: / Fire, burn; and, cauldron, bubble." When they are finished, Hecate, the queen of the Witches, enters together with three other Witches. The lines Hecate recites and the song the Witches sing are considered by some scholars to be non-Shakespearean.

After Hecate and the other Three Witches leave, Macbeth enters. He insists that the Witches answer his questions. It makes no difference to him, he says, whether or not the universe is totally destroyed in the process; he will have his answer. They agree, but first they inquire as to whether he would have the answer from them or from their masters; Macbeth prefers the latter. The Witches then throw into the boiling cauldron some unappetizing liquids: the blood of a sow who has eaten her young and the sweat that fell from a murderer as he was being hanged. This addition to the Witches' brew brings forth the apparition of an armed head. Macbeth is about to ask a question when the First Witch informs him that the Apparition knows his thought. The Apparition tells Macbeth to beware of Macduff, the Thane of Fife. The head then disappears. Macbeth thanks the armed head for cautioning him about Macduff and adds that this warning supports his own fear. Macbeth wishes to inquire further, but the First Witch tells him that the Apparition will not respond again. However, a stronger power will now appear.

The Second Apparition comes forth, and it is in the form of a bloody child. The Second Apparition advises Macbeth to be "bloody, bold, and resolute," for no one who was born of a woman can harm him. The Apparition disappears. Macbeth's comment on this information is that he need not fear Macduff (for Macduff is a man and all men are born of women). Macbeth, however, wishes to make "double sure"; he wishes to obliterate any trace of fear, and he says that he will kill Macduff anyway.

The Third Apparition now comes forth in the form of a crowned child with a tree in his hand. Macbeth asks who the Apparition is, but the witches merely tell him to listen. The Third Apparition advises Macbeth to be courageous ("lion-mettled") and proud, not to care about those who are dissatisfied or those who conspire against him, for Macbeth will never be defeated until the woods (called Birnam Wood) around his castle Dunsinane march toward the castle. The Third Apparition disappears. Macbeth says that it is impossible for a forest to move; the prediction is a good one. Macbeth now feels that he "Shall live the lease of Nature, pay his breath / To time, and mortal custom." That is, he feels he will die a natural death. However, he wishes to know one more thing: will Banquo's descendants ever rule Scotland? The Witches try to dissuade him from inquiring further, but Macbeth insists, whereupon the Witches call for a show; a show, they say, which will "grieve his heart."

There follows a procession of eight kings. The last of them holds a mirror. To anyone watching the procession from the front, the mirror makes it seem as though the line of kings stretches endlessly. Some of the kings carry "two-fold balls and treble sceptres." All of the kings in the procession resemble Banquo, and Banquo himself comes behind the line of eight, his hair caked with blood ("blood bolter'd"). He looks at Macbeth, smiles, and points at the procession; Macbeth takes these actions to mean that Banquo's descendants will, in fact, rule Scotland. Macbeth calls this pantomime a "horrible sight." To cheer him up the Witches perform a wild dance (an "antic round") and disappear. After they disappear, Macbeth says, "Let this pernicious hour / Stand aye accursed in the calendar!"

He calls for his attendant, who turns out to be Lennox. Macbeth asks Lennox whether the latter has seen the Witches. Lennox replies that he has not. Macbeth says that he heard a horse's gallop, and he wishes to know who went by. Lennox informs Macbeth that word was brought of Macduff's flight to England. "Time, thou anticipat'st my dread exploits," says Macbeth to himself. From now on, he continues, he will immediately do whatever his heart desires. And to turn his current wish into an act, he will make a surprise attack on Macduff's castle at Fife, and kill Macduff's wife, children, and any relative that might succeed him. Macbeth says that he will no longer boast. He will commit this act before his intention diminishes in strength. "But no more sights!" he says, apparently referring to what the Witches have shown him. He then asks to be led to the messengers, and Lennox and Macbeth exeunt.

Critical analysis. In his filmed version, Polanski here presents a cave full of nude witches, most of them old and physically repulsive, and some of them young. Their number suggests the multiplicity of witches at work in the world; and their varied ages intimate, since witches do not reproduce themselves, that sustained efforts at recruitment ensure the continuity of their kind. *In the Shakespearean text, however*, no more than six Witches and Hecate are called for, and there is of course no suggestion of nudity or, for that matter, of varied ages. *Another departure from the text occurs in the Schaefer filmed version*, which depicts the inebriated Macbeth sleeping and dreaming the cauldron scene, thus depreciating Shakespeare's emphasis on the supernatural.

Since Shakespeare's supernatural characters employ *shortened verse-forms*, one should note that the Witches speak in *seven-syllabled verse* with accents falling on syllables one, three, five, and seven. The brinded cat, the hedge-pig, and Harpier are animal and bird forms assumed by the familiar spirits of the Witches. One notices that the Witches never use even numbers; they are especially fond of threes, notable in their use of triplets, and when they say four (l. 2), it is by "Thrice, and once." *This marked tendency is to be thought of as a burlesque of the Trinity.*

Harpier is mentioned by name since he is leader of three devils.

The name, which seems to be of Shakespeare's invention, suggests the harpylike way in which the Sisters hover over the pot. Harpier, we gather, is a large owl that actually sounded on the earlier stage. Harpier is to be connected with II.ii.3: "It was the owl that shrieked." Lennox at II.iii.59–60 says: "The obscure bird / Clamor'd the livelong night." In II.iv.12–13 the owl hoots as Banquo is about to be killed, and the owl is mentioned suggestively in IV.ii.11 when the family of Macduff is endangered. *The owl-business has died down in modern performances* of *Macbeth* perhaps because of the danger of mimicry in an unruly audience.

In l. 3 a light stop, here a comma, after "cries" would mean that Harpier cries, "'Tis time, 'tis time." A heavy stop, *i.e.*, a semicolon (a period would be too heavy), signifies that Harpier cries; then the Third Witch interprets the cry, probably the sound of an owl. A light stop might be interpreted to mean that the familiar spirit of the Third Witch, unlike the spirits inhabiting the brinded cat and hedge-pig, is calling out his orders in English.

Ovid and Shakespeare. Among the ingredients of the Witches' brew the "Fillet of a fenny snake" (l. 12) is usually regarded as a slice; but Wood shows on the basis of Golding's translation of Ovid, usually acknowledged as influencing Shakespeare in the cauldron scene, that it is "the ribbon of its [a snake's] scarf-skin; and the snake is 'Fenny' because fen-bred."

Eight spurious lines? Hecate enters with three more Witches. She may be thought of as a devil because of the traditional notion that the gods of the heathen became devils. *Some scholars have regarded this part of the play as spurious*—J. Q. Adams, for example—removing from the text the first eight lines from the entrance of Hecate. *Some reasons for this view follow:* the speech is in iambic meter; Hecate does not bring the lunar venom which she mentions as to be used in "raising artificial sprites"; there are no "gains"; and l. 43 does not make good sense. The song "Black spirits" is in Middleton's *The*

Witch, and it was inserted in Sir William Davenant's Restoration version of *Macbeth*. Wood thinks that the line "By the pricking of my thumbs" derives from Reginald Scot's *The Discoverie of Witchcraft* (1584); if so, Shakespeare changed Scot's "tingling of the finger" into the coarser "pricking of my thumbs," preparing for the inevitable rhyme "comes." The line in any case conveys an ancient means of prognostication and so prepares for the advent of Macbeth.

Macbeth and Nature. Because Macbeth is to be obeyed (within limits) he is not obliged to employ circles and magical ceremonies to conjure devils. He delivers, as Holloway says, a formalized speech (ll. 50–61) rather like a curse in which he demands answers to his questions even if the cost is to be the destruction of Nature. Macbeth's speech is much like Northumberland's in *Henry IV, Part II*, I.i.153 ff. in theme and magniloquence: both men seem to think themselves outside Nature, which they would willingly let dissolve into chaos for merely selfish reasons. Macbeth thinks of Nature, as Edmund does in *King Lear*, as being in harmony with his career. This unorthodox view of Nature separates God and Nature. "Nature," as John F. Danby says in *Shakespeare's Doctrine of Nature*, "becomes given structure instead of normative pattern." Nature thus conceived excludes human values and reasonable norms. Nature has no intelligence, no connection with reason. Nature does not include man except on his bodily side; his mind is above it and free to manipulate it. Reason, instead of representing the ideal toward which men strive, becomes the means of satisfying men's appetites. *The orthodox Elizabethan view of Nature viewed it as a rational and benevolent arrangement. Nature is "bound to God."* Nature is nonmechanical; it is held together by Reason. Man's duty is to conform to custom, which represents codified Nature. Restraint is identified with Nature. Nature is identified with man's ability to reach, with the cooperation of his fellow men and circumstance, the realization of a large goal.

Richard Hooker's *Of the Laws of Ecclesiastical Polity* is a classic expression of this view, upon which Macbeth turns his back. At this point the Witches give Macbeth his choice between visions and prophecies, and with bare colloquial simplicity and fierce intensity he opts for the latter: "Call 'em; let me see 'em." The fact that these Witches have "masters" (l. 63) is sufficient to indicate that *they are not*, as Kittredge thought, *Norns*. The "masters" may be Paddock, Graymalkin, and Harpier; but one feels that superior devils are here referred to.

The First Apparition, an Armed Head, really means the beheading of Macbeth by Macduff, but the audience is not aware of this until Act V. That Booth had the armed head made up like Macbeth readily brought the matter home to his audience, but it is doubtful that Macbeth would notice this. Macbeth never again mentions the First Apparition, but he twists the Second and Third Apparitions to his own purpose. Heaven keeps him from making anything of a connection between the First Apparition and his own head brought in on a pole by Macduff. It will be noticed that Witches thrice in this scene prevent Macbeth from asking questions of the Apparitions: the devils, charmed by the Witches, have shown Macbeth things that will kill him, and they are not bound to tell him the truth.

Necromancy and King James. The Second Apparition represents Macduff though in a character not known to Macbeth at present. The line "More potent than the first" really means that Macduff is "more potent" than Macbeth. Necromancy in the strict sense is used in that devils enter exhumed bodies rather than take the forms of human beings. Such was James's view. The two children are presumably unbaptized infants (cf. ll. 30–31). The disseveredhead, the bloody child, and the crowned child should tell Macbeth how to extinguish Macduff's revolt; but actually they ambiguously foretell his death, his killer, and his supplanters. By "assurance double" (l. 83) Macbeth means that by killing Macduff, he will put it out of harm's power to reach him unless Fate breaks the law of birth and the law of death.

The Third Apparition, a crowned child, enters with a tree in his hand signifying not only the later march from Birnam Wood to Dunsinane but also the bloody and unnatural giving way to nature as orthodoxy conceived. The word "Dunsinane," by the way, is pronounced in IV.i.93 with stress on the penult in Scottish fashion; in Act V it is stressed eight times on the antipenult, English fashion. *It is valuable to note the difference between Macbeth at III.iv.122–26, where he as a man of conscience thinks that even stones and trees speak out to expose foul murder, and Macbeth in this scene where he is convinced (ll. 94–96) that no one can "impress the forest, bid the tree / Unfix his earth-bound root."* He cannot see, as William Free observes, that if a power can move trees to expose murder, it can move a forest for the same purpose. Macbeth is so impressed with the visions and willing to accept the oracles that he falls to rhyming in ll. 94 ff. There follows in l. 97 a choice for editors between "Rebellion's dead," the Folio reading, and Theobald's emendation "Rebellious head." As a reference to Banquo, the original makes excellent sense and links with Banquo in ll. 100–103: Banquo may rise again in his son, his followers, and supporters.

Macbeth's pleasure in these prophecies is speedily removed by the show of kings and the smiling Ghost of Banquo. A notable difference between the Apparitions and the kings is that the former exist whereas the kings, according to King James, are technically a "sight"—they are "an impression in the air, shown to the eyes, deluding the senses, but nonexistent." Bradbrook and Paul emphasize the topicality of the show of kings.

An interesting question is why Shakespeare omits Mary Stuart from the eight—Robert II, Robert III, and the six Jameses–since Mary was sovereign for twenty-five years between James V and James VI, *i.e.*, James I of England. The prophecy to Banquo is "Thou shalt get kings," and Mary was a queen. In *Macbeth* female beings tempt to evil and unwise deeds, and it would be imprudent to introduce a queen into the Stuart dynasty. *For reasons of state and of religion it would have been inappropriate to remind the sovereign of his mother* (executed by order of

Queen Elizabeth) *and the audience of the unhappy Mary.*

The kings are connected to Banquo by the family characteristic of abundant hair (cf. III.iv.50). There is a discrepancy between the Folio's calling for Banquo to have a glass, *i.e.*, a magic mirror, in his hand and editorial policy in placing the glass in the hand of the eighth king. Probably the last of the eight kings should enter with the glass, Banquo's Ghost standing by and watching the procession with pleasure. A gauze to "soften the glare of reality" might well be introduced here into a stage version.

Banquo and Elizabeth II. It is interesting to note that the verse "Will the line stretch out to the crack of doom?" has relevance to the current sovereign, for Queen Elizabeth II is descended from King James I. The "twofold balls" perhaps allude to King James's being crowned at Scone and at Westminster, and the "treble sceptres" may allude to King James's being crowned King of Great Britain, France, and Ireland, or perhaps to his rule over England, Scotland, and Ireland. The kings disappear into the exiguous air which is their substance.

The First Witch, speaking in ll. 125 ff. (in a manner strongly intimating interpolation by another writer), suggests, contrary to the mood of great tragedy, that Macbeth needs to be cheered up and calls for a dance of the Six Witches to music. Clifford Davidson and others have conjectured that in the Globe performance of *Macbeth* the dances at this point were adapted from Ben Jonson's *Masque of Queenes* (1609), in which six grotesque hags dance "contrary to the custome of Men." It is difficult indeed to think that Macbeth would patiently sit through the beldam ballet and then, upon the disappearance of the *danseuses*, exclaim "Where are they? Gone?" Generally, as ll. 138–39 intimate, Macbeth's second interview with the Witches suggests a falling away of his resolution.

Lennox's position in this play needs defining. He is one of Macbeth's most trusted advisors, yet we find in III.vi that he is a ringleader against Macbeth. He has concealed from Macbeth knowledge of Macduff's flight from the king. Macbeth evidently trusts him, for Lennox hears the king's plan for revenge against Macduff.

ACT IV, SCENE ii

Plot summary. This scene takes place in Macduff's castle at Fife. Lady Macduff, her son, and Ross enter. Lady Macduff is speaking to Ross. She does not understand why her husband has run away from Scotland. "His flight was madness," she says. She implies that even though Macduff is not a traitor, his fear makes him look like one. Ross tells Lady Macduff that she cannot know whether it was fear or wisdom that made her husband run. But, she questions, how can his flight be wise when he leaves his wife and children in a place from which he himself runs away. "All is the fear, and nothing is the love . . . ," she comments. Macduff's flight, she insists, was unreasonable. Ross tells Lady Macduff that her husband is a wise and trustworthy man. He understands the cruel times in which men "float upon a wild and violent sea . . . ." Ross, however, breaks off the conversation to say that he must leave. But he will soon be back. He comforts Lady Macduff by saying that things at their worst will either come to an end or improve. He gives his blessing to young Macduff, whom Lady Macduff calls "fatherless." Ross feels he cannot prevent himself from weeping, and so he departs at once.

An amusingly pathetic dialogue now ensues between Lady Macduff and her son. Lady Macduff says to her son that his father is dead. "How will you live?" she asks. He will live as the birds do, he replies. "Poor bird!" she calls him, and she hopes that he need never fear a trap as birds fear it. The son now reverts to their former conversation and says that he does not believe that his father is dead. His mother insists that his father is dead, and they joke a bit about a consequent search for another husband. The son then asks, "Was my father a traitor, mother?" Lady Macduff replies that his father was. The son now asks, "What is a traitor?" "Why, one that swears and lies," she answers. The question arises whether all that swear and lie must be hanged. To Lady Macduff's affirmative response, the son says that "the liars and swearers are fools." They are fools because there are more of them than there are honest men. If the liars and swearers were smart, they would band together and hang the honest man. Lady Macduff now returns to her former theme: "But how wilt thou do for a father?" The boy still does not believe that his father is dead. If his father were really dead, the boy insists, she would weep for him. A messenger suddenly enters. He is not known to Lady Macduff, he tells her, although he is looking out for her honor. He warns her to run away, for danger is fast approaching her. He blesses her, says that he dare not stay longer, and exits. Lady Macduff exclaims that she does not know where to run. "I have done no harm," she says. But, she reflects, in this world it is often praiseworthy to do harm; to do good is often thought to be "dangerous folly." Why, then, does she bother saying that she has done no harm?

Murderers suddenly interrupt her. "Where is your husband?" one Murderer asks. Lady Macduff replies that she hopes that he is in no place so unholy that he can be found by the Murderer (who, she implies, would ordinarily frequent only places that are damned). The Murderer says that Macduff is a traitor. Macduff's son cries, "Thou liest, thou shag hair'd villain!" At this the Murderer stabs the boy, who tells his mother to run away. The scene ends with Lady Macduff running off the stage crying "Murder!" followed by the Murderers.

Critical analysis. This scene advances the plot by showing how swiftly Macbeth carries out his revenge against Lady Macduff and her offspring. The dramatic effect of omitting this scene from stage from representations is unwarrantedly to improve the character of Macbeth and to prevent us from seeing domestic affection. *Little Macduff is rendered interesting by his* *mixture of insight and naivete, his attempt to confute his mother, his mother's addressing him as if he were a person of importance, his serious response to his mother's facetious touches, and his gallantry.*

At this point Macduff has done nothing treasonable; and Lady Macduff, though thoroughly incensed at his departure, which presumably the husband has not discussed with his wife lest he implicate her, does not really believe that her husband is a traitor. Although she appears to be *an idiot in the Greek sense of being unversed in political affairs*, she has premonitions of disaster. In her conversation with Ross she points to the diminutive wren that, unlike Macduff, will fight for its young: Elizabethans were in the habit of seeing nature, both animate and inanimate, as reflecting human emotions, moods, and attitudes. In saying "All is the fear, and nothing is the love" (l. 12), she draws upon I John, 4, 18 "perfect love casteth out fear." Shakespeare's extensive use of the Bible, by the way, is based upon the popular Geneva Version and the Bishops' Bible. Ross, in trying to comfort her, speaks of "The fits o' th' season," intimating Macbeth's accesses of murderous passion. This kind of imagery suggests that Macbeth's tyranny, manifesting itself by fits and starts rather than by a steady, grinding malevolence, is beginning to ebb. Unsuccessful in his attempts at consolation, Ross abruptly leaves.

Use of you and thou. In the conversation between Lady Macduff and her son, she uses the formal "you" in the mock solemnity of "Sirrah, your father's dead, / And what will you do now?" The boy always responds with the formal "you," indicating his class and nurture. When Lady Macduff is pleased with his answers, she allows her affectionate nature to flow towards him by the use of "thou" and "thee." Generally one apprehends that *since Elizabethan children were thought of as miniature adults*, little Macduff is a worthy scion of his line, what with his common sense and his trust in his father; and his wretched death from an Elizabethan point of view is more pitiable on this account.

Who sends the Messenger? A Messenger enters with a warning to Lady Macduff that she and her children should depart their castle immediately. It is possible, though we do not know it, that he has come from Lady Macbeth, from Lennox, or from some friend of the Macduffs who has learned Macbeth's purposes. Simply his presence and his mission remind one that Macbeth has not been able to suborn even the lowlier elements of the Scottish population. His reference to "little ones" in l. 69 is a reminiscence of Matt. 18, 6 wherein a dreadful retribution is threatened for "whosoever shall offend one of these little ones which believe in me."

At this point the Murderers enter. *Polanski* has Young Macduff bathing—thus he *connects with effect a nude bloody child previously seen in the Witches' cauldron.* Lady Macduff, seeing them, cries, "What are these faces?" The villains' shaggy hair marks them as being Elizabethan professional ruffians, men of a different class than the desperate gentlemen who dispatched Banquo. Accent would be suitably vulgarized. The First Murderer's question "Where is your husband?" is rhetorical rather than genuine, for he must say something. The gallant Young Macduff attempts to face him down with "Thou li'st, thou shag-ear'd villain," but the boy is horribly murdered in the sight of the audience. Shakespeare as an Elizabethan playwright is not, in the matter of onstage murder, in the tradition derived from the ancient Greeks who declined to represent bloodshed before the eyes of the audience. Macbeth's purpose is apparently an attempt to prevent other thanes from following Macduff's example, and the Macduffs are killed because they share the blood of the husband and father.

ACT IV, SCENE iii

Plot summary. The scene takes place at the palace of King Edward of England. Malcolm and Macduff enter. To Malcolm's remark that Macduff and he go to a deserted spot and weep out their sadness, Macduff replies that they ought rather to hold in their hands their deadly swords and conquer their native land. There every morning "New widows howl, new orphans cry; new sorrows / Strike heaven on the face . . . ." Malcolm replies in effect that he does not trust Macduff. "He [Macbeth] hath not touch'd you yet" (that is, he has not hurt you yet) continues Malcolm. He suggests that perhaps Macduff is looking for a reward from Macbeth by luring Malcolm to Scotland. Macduff answers, "I am not treacherous." "But Macbeth is," says Malcolm: a good man may not be able to resist orders from a king. But Malcolm then begs Macduff's pardon. Malcolm says that his thoughts cannot change Macduff's nature. Even though some good people may change, not all good people change. Macduff (seeing that Malcolm is hesitant about his proposals) says that he, Macduff, has lost his hopes (for an invasion of Scotland). But it is in Scotland that Malcolm finds his reasons for doubting Macduff. Why did Macduff suddenly leave his wife and children, asks Malcolm. Malcolm begs Macduff not to take the question as implying Macduff's dishonor but rather Malcolm's caution for his own life. Apparently feeling the hopelessness of persuading a suspicious man of one's innocence, Macduff says that his country must continue in its ruin. He adds that he would not be suspected as a deceiver for all of Scotland and the rich Orient combined.

Macduff is about to leave but Malcolm tells Macduff not to be offended, for Malcolm has spoken not merely in fear of Macduff. Malcolm believes his country is suffering, that there would be Scotsmen who would come over to his side. From "gracious England" he has received offers of help. But despite all of this, when he has conquered the tyrant Macbeth, Scotland would suffer more from Macbeth's successor than it is suffering now. To Macduff's question, "What should he be?" Malcolm replies that he is talking about himself, who, in the course of time, would make Macbeth appear pure. Macduff replies that no one could be worse than Macbeth. Malcolm says that he knows Macbeth is "Luxurious [lustful], avaricious, false, deceitful, /

Sudden [violent], malicious, smacking of every sin / That has a name . . . ." However, he continues, not all the women of Scotland can ever satisfy *his* lust; it would be better for Macbeth to reign. Macduff replies that such lust is tyrannical and has caused the fall of many kings; but Malcolm should not hesitate to take the kingdom that belongs to him. For undoubtedly enough women will find the greatness of kingship sufficient lure so that he will be satisfied. But Malcolm goes on to speak of another fault. He is so avaricious that he would invent quarrels with his good and loyal subjects only to obtain their wealth. This is worse than lust, says Macduff; but Scotland has riches enough to quench Malcolm's desire. Lust and avarice are bearable when other virtues ("graces") are taken into account. But, Malcolm answers, he has no other virtues. He has no desire for the virtues which are fit for a king; such virtues as "justice, verity, temperance, stableness, / Bounty, perseverance, mercy, lowliness, / Devotion, patience, courage, fortitude." Instead, if he had the power, he would "Pour the sweet milk of concord into hell, / Uproar the universal peace, confound / All unity on earth."

Macduff replies that the kind of man that Malcolm describes is not only unfit to govern but also unfit to live. He wonders when his nation will once more see "wholesome days." Now a bloody usurper is on the throne and the rightful occupant is self-accused in villainy. Macduff goes on, apparently trying to understand how it came about that Malcolm is so evil, for he talks of Malcolm's parents who were very holy. Macduff bids good-bye to Malcolm and adds that what he has learned of Malcolm's character has in effect banished him from Scotland (for no invasion will occur, and he cannot otherwise return).

Malcolm once more holds back Macduff. Malcolm says that Macduff has shown himself to be a man of integrity and has erased Malcolm's suspicion of him. Macbeth, Malcolm says, had tried to trick Malcolm into returning to Scotland by sending men who acted as Macduff did at first. Malcolm has had to use "modest wisdom" to discern the true man from the false. But he knows now that Macduff is honest, and he says that all the evil character he has given himself is untrue. The first lies that he has ever told have been about himself. His true self is ready to obey the commands of Macduff and of his country. Also, Old Siward, the Earl of Northumberland, has already started for Scotland with ten thousand men. "Now," continues Malcolm, "we'll together . . . ." Malcolm asks Macduff why the latter is silent. Macduff replies that he is confused by the quick reversal of things.

A doctor enters and Malcolm stops the discussion with Macduff; they will continue it later, he says. Malcolm now addresses the doctor, asking him whether the king (King Edward) is coming out. The doctor replies in the affirmative: a group of sick people are waiting to be cured by the king. Their illnesses cannot be cured by the art of medicine, but King Edward's hand has been given such holiness that when the sick people are touched by him, they are cured. Malcolm thanks the doctor, who then exits. Macduff asks Malcolm what illness the doctor is talking about. Malcolm replies that the illness is called the evil. He has often seen the good King Edward perform this miraculous cure. How Edward has asked heaven for this miraculous power only Edward knows. All Malcolm knows is that people sick with the evil, a disease that causes swelling and ulcers, are cured by Edward and cannot be cured by doctors. It is said that this healing power will be inherited by Edward's successors. With this ability to heal he has the "heavenly gift of prophecy; / And sundry blessings," which indicate that he is "full of grace."

Ross enters. Macduff recognizes him immediately, but Malcolm has some difficulty in doing so apparently because Malcolm has not seen Ross for a long time. Macduff asks Ross how things are going in Scotland. Ross replies that things are very bad; the country cannot "Be called our mother, but our grave." Violence and death are commonplace. Malcolm asks what has given the most recent cause for grief. Ross answers that anyone attempting to report a crime an hour old as the newest cause of grief would be ridiculed, for every minute brings new ones.

"How does my wife?" inquires Macduff. "Why, well," replies Ross. "And all my children?" is Macduff's next question, to which Ross answers, "Well, too." Macduff then asks whether Macbeth has not harassed Macduff's family. "No," says Ross; "they were well at peace, when I did leave 'em." Macduff tells Ross not to be so stingy in details about the family; he wishes to know how they are. Instead of answering him, Ross says that when he came here to bring his sad news, a rumor went about that many good men had taken up arms against Macbeth. Ross believes this to be true, because Macbeth had his army mobilized. "Now is the time of help," he says. Malcolm's appearance in Scotland would cause many, including women, to fight and rid themselves of their troubles. Malcolm tells Ross about the forthcoming invasion, which will be aided by Siward, than whom no older nor better soldier can be found in Christendom. Ross says that he wishes his news were as good. Macduff asks whether the news concerns all of them or one of them. Ross says that all virtuous men must share the grief of his news, but mainly the news concerns Macduff. The latter requests that it be given to him quickly. After apologizing for the necessity of bringing Macduff such a report, Ross tells him that his wife and children have been "savagely slaughtered."

Probably because he is weeping, Macduff pulls his hat over his eyes. After an expression of shock, Malcolm tells Macduff that the latter should not have pulled his hat over his eyes. If a man does not speak out his grief, Malcolm continues, his heart breaks. Macduff merely asks, "My children too?" To this question Ross replies, "Wife, children, servants, all / That could be found." Macduff cries, "And I must be from thence!" That is, he is exclaiming over the bitterness of his absence from his castle at the time of the attack. Evidently unable completely to absorb the situation, he once more inquires, "My wife kill'd too?" Ross tells Macduff that what he has said is true. Malcolm tells Macduff to cure his grief with revenge upon Macbeth. "He has no children," says Macduff, probably referring to Macbeth. Still unable to accept the terrible facts, Macduff now asks whether all of his children were killed. "O Hell-kite!" he exclaims. "All?" Were all the children and their mother killed at once? Malcolm tells Macduff to fight against his grief like a man. Macduff says that he will do so; "But I must also feel it as a man . . . ." He then says, "Sinful Macduff!" All his family were killed, he feels, not for their original sin (for they were so innocent, it would seem, they had none) but for his. Having cried out his grief, he can accept the horrible facts: ". . . heaven rest them now!" he says. Malcolm tells Macduff to "let grief / Convert to anger." Macduff says that he could weep now and brag. Instead, he prays to heaven to bring him as soon as possible face to face with the "fiend of Scotland." If Macbeth escapes, may heaven forgive Macbeth. Malcolm says that Macduff's words are manly. Malcolm now tells his countrymen to come along to the king (King Edward); "our power [army] is ready," he says, all they require is leave from the king. "Macbeth is ripe for shaking," Malcolm says in the concluding lines of the scene, "and the powers above / Put on their instruments." (The last words mean that the forces of heaven are arming themselves.)

Critical analysis. This scene, based on Holinshed's *Chronicle*, concerns Malcolm's testing of Macduff's loyalty: the fact that such an examination is necessary shows the far-flung currents of Macbeth's depravity. *The Romantic view that the scene is tedious is wrong* because a normal audience would wish to know whether Malcolm is qualified to be named King of Scotland and whether or not his relationship with his chief thane, Macduff, is good. Although Malcolm is decidedly awkward in depicting himself as a paragon of vice, he shows that he has learned the Renaissance rule *qui dissimulare nescit, regnare nescit*, "He who does not know how to dissimulate does not know how to rule." He presents evidence that in truly knowing his friends and his enemies, he will excel his father, who admittedly did not know how to find "the mind's construction in the face." Since *Macbeth* is a tragedy and since Shakespeare's tragedies (unlike his histories) are more basically concerned with morality than with politics, one should say with Herbert Coursen that *this scene exhibits a future King of Scotland whose fundamental virtue is aided and strengthened by his political skill.* Not only that. The scene is resonant with suggestions that *Heaven and Malcolm are in alliance*: his return to Scotland with "goodly thousands" will be by sanction of the indomitable "powers above" which "put on their instruments" to cleanse Scotland of Macbeth.

Malcolm's suspicion. Malcolm has a reasonable suspicion of Macduff because of the thane's desertion of his defenseless wife and children, and it will be observed that Macduff does not answer the Prince's question on this point. *Nineteenth-century audiences, regarding this matter as painful and unnatural, omitted the scene from representation; but, as Bradbrook suggests, the twentieth century, well acquainted with* agents provocateurs *and the uprooting of families for political reasons, has a better understanding of this part of the plot.* In Holinshed the scene loses force because both Malcolm and Macduff know of Macbeth's murder of Macduff's family from the beginning. One gathers that Macduff concealed his intentions of flight from Scotland from his fellow thanes to prevent them from implication, which would expose them to Macbeth's rage. Malcolm's method of testing Macduff is by making provocative remarks such as suggesting that Macduff may have foul motives for leaving wife and children in Scotland, and by heaping undeserved obloquy upon himself, such as saying what he will do with the Scottish nobles' estates if he should become king.

Malcolm begins by stating the need to weep; Macduff counters, using the figure of hand-to-hand combat to protect the body of a fallen comrade, by asserting the need for military action. Malcolm declares Macbeth a "tyrant": *Elizabethans carefully distinguished*, as W. A. Armstrong points out, *between tyrants who held usurped thrones and bad kings who by lawful heredity had been rightfully anointed*—the former could be attacked openly or sub rosa, the latter were to be religiously endured. Macbeth is clearly a tyrant since he is no son to Duncan and has been wrongly anointed although the play admittedly offers no intimation of the latter point. In l. 15 the Folio reads "discerne," but editors, following Theobald, generally read "You may deserve of him through me." But if we assume that Malcolm would not broach the matter of material advancement to Macduff, as we should, the Folio reading had better be retained. Malcolm in the midst of l. 20 reads grief and horror in Macduff's face— an implicit stage-direction. In ll. 23–24 Malcolm says, in Dr. Johnson's paraphrase, "I do not say that your virtuous appearance proves you are a traitor; for virtue must wear its proper form, though that form be counterfeited by villainy." Malcolm centers his mind on the never-explained reason for Macduff's leaving of wife and children to the wolfish Macbeth: specifically he fears an understanding between the tyrant and Macduff. Since no explanation is forthcoming, he proceeds to dishonor himself in a highly concrete fashion to observe how Macduff reacts.

"The man behind Macbeth." Essentially he recites and exaggerates Macbeth's villainies except that, as Bradley has pointed out, lechery and avarice are not properly charged to Macbeth's account. Sir James Fergusson is of the opinion that this coloring may derive from the sixteenth-century James Stuart, whom Sir James styles "the man behind Macbeth." Macduff is not greatly disturbed by Macbeth's lechery or by Malcolm's magnified imputation of himself as being so stained, for princes were commonly given to this vice. What appalls Macduff are the evidences of avarice, pride, ambition, self-seeking, deceit— vices that do not disappear with the disappearance of youth. Malcolm continues in ll. 91 ff. in cataloging his vices, thereby defining by negatives what a good king should be and what Malcolm actually is. Malcolm says that he would "Uproar the universal peace," a line that must have, per contra, pleased King James, who affected himself in the role of peacemaker and who was desirous of Christian unity. Bradbrook suggests that James, who himself practiced dissimulation with the Ruthven gang of kidnappers when he was eighteen, would have watched with personal interest Malcolm's provocation of Macduff. This list, by which Malcolm marks himself a veritable cesspool of

villainy, has the improbable effect of causing Macduff to expostulate that Malcolm is not only unfit to govern but even to live: Malcolm's true character must have been known to Macduff when Malcolm left Scotland; more important, Macduff has been told the Confessor trusts Malcolm (ll. 43–44).

Macduff's reactions. It is interesting to note that Macduff shows no ambition to push himself into Malcolm's place when Malcolm admits practicing every crime under the sun. Macduff does not go to the length of denying Malcolm's legal right to the throne: presumably Malcolm would be an evil but legitimate king, in Macduff's view, who would elicit religious endurance from those subjects not in position to exile themselves. Macduff contrasts Malcolm with his "most sainted" father and with his mother, who "Died every day she liv'd," meaning that she died to worldly desires (cf. Paul's "I die daily," I Cor. 15, 31) every day of her life. Since historical record does not warrant the saintliness of Duncan's wife, one gathers that Shakespeare, again desiring to gratify King James, transferred St. Margaret's reputation to her mother-in-law. St. Margaret was Malcolm's wife and had a strong influence on his policy, bringing it about that Scottish kings should be anointed by the Pope. It is chiefly the memory of Malcolm's father and mother that convinces Macduff that Malcolm is not speaking truly of himself.

"An excellent team." Thus Malcolm passes his examination, not trusting at first even the ingenuous Macduff (by comparison with Macbeth); and Macduff passes his. One apprehends that Malcolm and Macduff will make an excellent team because Malcolm lacks force but possesses prudence, and Macduff has force aplenty but is somewhat naive. It must be said, however, that Malcolm has sufficient force to advance on Scotland with Old Siward and ten thousand men. One's estimate of Malcolm's prudence is raised by learning (ll. 117–20) that he has declined Macbeth's blandishments aimed at luring him back to Scotland. Line 118 lengthens the time since Malcolm took refuge at the court of the Confessor. Then Malcolm exonerates himself of the vices he has claimed and makes Macduff commander of the forces against Macbeth.

A Doctor enters with notice that a band of suppliants possessed of scrofula await the royal touch of the Confessor for healing. This passage provides an interval of time before the arrival of Ross with news of the murder of Macduff's wife and children, and it serves as a substitute for the appearance of the Confessor onstage, which could encumber the action. The business of healing "the King's evil" is introduced into the play for several reasons. It shows that Malcolm by virtue of his healing touch is the true King of Scotland even though he has this power only by association with Saint Edward the Confessor and even though he does not use it in this place: since the audience is in no doubt about Malcolm's legitimacy and purity it is not necessary for him to validate this power. *The beneficent supernatural spoken of here contrasts with the evil supernatural of the Witches just as the sainted Edward contrasts with Macbeth*. Knights points out that the healing imagery contrasts with the disease imagery prominent in Act V. Finally, the entrance of Ross with his evil news comes more dramatically after this quiet scene than it would after one with heavy action. Curiously, the matter of touching was viewed with disfavor in contemporary Scotland, and James shared this view. James, upon becoming King of England, was induced to take up touching (in a much modified ceremony) as showing his legitimacy. He used no angel (a coin); he declined to make the sign of the cross; he held the Protestant view that miracles had ceased. The King was supposed to say (the service is found in old prayerbooks) "Le Roy vous touche, Dieu vous guery" (the king touches you, the Lord heals you). By the use of this expression the King relieved his mind on the score of endorsing superstition, and his patients would not know what he said. The English were trying to persuade the King to resume the Elizabethan practice of touching, and *Macbeth* gave him a nudge in this direction. Malcolm does not say that he has taken Saint Edward as his model, for to do so would be priggish; but he has obviously done so. Edward is not mentioned here by name, for he is a mysterious presence; furthermore, Shakespeare does not wish to throw Malcolm into too much obscurity which would naturally come if Saint Edward is to be too prominent.

Ross's ambiguity. Ross enters. Although Malcolm does not know him by name, he recognizes him by his costume as a Scot. Macduff, who has been away from home for a time before Macbeth started tyrannizing the countryside, asks about his wife and family. Ross is hesitant about conveying the worst news and uses the ambiguous "well," meaning that Lady Macduff and her children are in Heaven (cf. *Antony and Cleopatra*, II.v.32–33). Then he openly states in a manner neither too short nor too long, "Your castle is surpris'd; your wife and babes / Savagely slaughter'd." For him to have used softness would have been cruel; to have been graphic, in the manner of a messenger in a Greek tragedy, would have been cruel too. *For Ross to pun on "deer" (l. 206) at this tragic moment is something for which Shakespeare was condemned by neoclassicists;* but the ancient Greeks, who sometimes permitted word play on similar occasions, suggest its naturalness. The effect of this shocking news on Macduff is to harden him against Macbeth and to bring closer the final reckoning. Here we learn what previously we have sensed—the Satanic Macbeth has no children, which Macduff assuredly does not utter because of the removal of the possibility of exact retaliation: the child Lady Macbeth mentions in I.vii must have died in infancy. Macduff, saying "Naught that I am" (wicked man that I am), regards the cause of this atrocity as a judgment of Heaven on his sins; yet despite what he says, and remembering Lady Macduff's describing her husband's flight as "madness," we are not expected to blame Macduff. Macduff cries, ". . . if he scape, Heaven forgive him too!" meaning "If I let him escape, I will not only forgive him myself, but I pray God to forgive him also." He is obviously hopeful not only of Macbeth's death but of his condemnation to Hell (cf. *Hamlet*, III.iii.73–95). The scene ends, as blank-verse scenes in Shakespeare's plays commonly do, with the finality of a couplet.

ACT V, SCENE i

Plot summary. The scene occurs in a room at Dunsinane. Except for the last nine lines the scene is in prose. A Doctor and a Gentlewoman who waits on Lady Macbeth enter. The Doctor addresses the Gentlewoman. He has stayed awake with the latter for two nights, but he has not seen what she reported to him. He asks her when Lady Macbeth last walked in her sleep. The Gentlewoman replies that, since Macbeth ("his majesty") went into the field to fight, she has seen Lady Macbeth get up from bed, put on her dressing-gown ("night gown"), write on some paper, seal it, and return to bed. All the time she did this, Lady Macbeth was fast asleep. The Doctor says it is a disturbance of nature when one is simultaneously awake and asleep. He then asks what Lady Macbeth has said. The Gentlewoman refuses to tell, even to the Doctor, because she has no witness to support her statement.

As the Gentlewoman speaks, Lady Macbeth enters holding a lighted candle, which, the Gentlewoman informs the Doctor, Lady Macbeth has at her bedside all the time. From the conversation of the two observers, we learn that the queen is sleep walking; her eyes are open "but their sense are shut." She is also making the motion of washing her hands. The Gentlewoman has seen her mistress do this sometimes for a quarter of an hour.

Until she exits, Lady Macbeth speaks a number of disconnected phrases and sentences. Most of Lady Macbeth's remarks refer to incidents which have been dramatized in the play; a listener might infer from her remarks a soul tortured by the guilty acts of its owner. The two listeners do make this inference about Lady Macbeth and express their shock at what they have been forced to conclude. When Lady Macbeth leaves, the Doctor indicates that rumors are flying about of "unnatural deeds" committed by the ruling couple. Guilty minds, he says, will relieve themselves of their secrets by telling them to their pillows, which do not really hear. He asks God to forgive them all. He tells the Gentlewoman to look after her mistress and to remove from the latter any means of self-harm. He ends with "I think but dare not speak." The Gentlewoman bids the Doctor good night, and they exeunt.

Critical analysis. Lady Macbeth has been portrayed quite variously in her last appearance in the play. Henry Irving wrote to Ellen Terry, "The sleepwalking scene will be beautiful too the moment you are in it—*but* Lady Macbeth should certainly have the appearance of having got out of bed, to which she is returning when she goes off. The hair to my mind should be wild and disordered, and the whole appearance as distraught as possible, and disordered. . . ." The Polanski filmed version, sponsored by Hugh Hefner of *Playboy*, presents a nude Lady Macbeth—"Lady MacBuff," as she was described in the London *Times* of Oct. 26, 1971. In the Kurosawa filming entitled *Throne of Blood*, Lady Macbeth's pregnancy, announced when Macbeth is about to take possession of the throne, renders her ambitious; and a miscarriage drives her insane. This notable departure from the text, as Gerlach says, gives "social and biological excuses for what can only be laid to unfathomable greed in Shakespeare's Macbeth."

If Lady Macbeth holds herself in hand until the sleepwalking scene, it would have the advantage of surprise except for the brief interchange between the Doctor and the Waiting Gentlewoman. But one could characterize her on the basis of *the hint in III.ii.4–7* as growing weary, sick of blood, and apprehensive of further murders; this would somewhat blunt the shock of the sleepwalking scene. A headstrong actress would perhaps attempt a *coup de* théâtre here, but it would destroy the *contrast between Lady Macbeth's slow weakening and Macbeth's slow hardening.*

The stain of blood. Lady Macbeth's malaise exhibits the following *symptoms*: she walks, speaks prose, and even writes in her sleep; and her *theme*, as she rehearses fragmentary reminiscences of murders, is her blood guilt seen visibly on her hands which she continually washes without effect. The idea of bloodstained hands probably came to Shakespeare from Pilate's washing his hands of the guilt of the Saviour's death; but Beatrice points out that in *Gesta Romanorum* there is a story of "a woman of queenly station and hitherto of blameless report who in the interests of her own security murders an innocent person. The blood of her victim falls upon her hand, and although she makes repeated efforts to remove the stain, it remains. Oppressed by the burden of her guilty secret, she finally makes confession to a priest and the stain vanishes."

One gathers that Macbeth has been in the field (l. 4) against his rebellious subjects since the time before Ross went to England (see IV.iii.185). The Doctor and the Gentlewoman prepare us for Lady Macbeth's strange entry. She carries a taper concerning which Bradley comments: "The failure of nature in Lady Macbeth is marked by her fear of darkness; 'She has light by her continually.'" Although the Gentlewoman knows that Lady Macbeth cannot see, she tells the Doctor to "stand close": this act is instinctive, and it gives the center of the stage to Lady Macbeth. *Lady Macbeth speaks in prose because Shakespeare uses this medium for abnormal mental states* as, for example, when Hamlet is acting madly, when Ophelia and Lear are insane, and when Othello in IV.i is virtually in this condition. The regular rhythms of verse, Shakespeare may have thought, ill accord with a mind that has lost its balance. It would be dramatically unwise for Lady Macbeth to speak with sepulchral solemnity and to appear the incarnation of Nemesis, for she is a living woman disturbed by fear and guilt.

Evidence of conscience. Her sleepwalking is probably a sign of demonic possession in the form of demonic bloodletting. Evidence for this view is the lines "Come to my woman's breasts, / And take my milk for gall, you murth'ring ministers" (I.v.47–48). Milk was in Elizabethan physiological thought an alternate form of blood. Shakespeare, who usually shrinks from depiction or suggestion of the utterly abominable, delineated Joan of Arc in *I Henry VI* as a witch who lost blood to demons

(V.iii.14). This distressful situation, by its diminution of Lady Macbeth's blood together with the thickening dregs of melancholy, causes her mind to totter. Most of her words seem to be directed to the absent Macbeth. Her revulsion from the murders, as well as her thinking herself able at some time in her life to have a child, is good evidence of her possession of a conscience however much seared. She says, "one—two—why then 'tis time to do't," which intimates that Duncan was murdered soon after two in the morning. "What need we fear who knows it, when none can call our pow'r to accompt?" appears to mean that law and tyrants have no part with each other.

A new contribution to scholarship. Reference to Duncan's blood is a hitherto uncommented-upon compliment to King James because old men in Shakespeare's time and in his plays conventionally have little blood: Duncan's abundant blood is a testimony to a life of blessing and virtue beyond nature's course; it signifies that he could have begotten male offspring who would have closely resembled him (rather than their mother); and, of course, it tends to certify both Malcolm and Duncan's line generally. Whether the Doctor understands the reference to the "old man" is unclear, but he certainly knows that the murder of Lady Macduff is weighing upon Lady Macbeth's conscience. In l. 50—"Here's the smell of the blood still"—"smell" rather than "blood" should be emphasized because the spot, Lady Macbeth thinks, has been removed at last. The expression is reminiscent of Cassandra smelling blood and vapors from the tomb in the palace of Atrides in Aeschylus' *Agamemnon*, ll. 1306–11. At this point in *Macbeth*, Mrs. Siddons, one of the great actresses in this role, passed her hands before her nose as if she perceived a foul smell, eliciting the following comment from Leigh Hunt, ". . . she should have shuddered and looked in despair, as recognizing the strain on her soul." Alice Fox points out that Lady Macbeth, being a woman, is more aware than her husband of the smell of blood, Macbeth being preoccupied with its sight. Lady Macbeth's dreams reconstruct something of the terror and coloring (hands, water, blood, and darkness) of the entire play. To have a physician hear them, as Kocher suggests, is to show that her death is not caused by natural melancholy, nor by insanity, but by conscience, which is beyond the power of medicine. If the Doctor had been allowed competence, he would have obscured the point that Shakespeare wishes to make. Lady Macbeth would like to confuse conscience and melancholy (I.v.43 ff.), but the Doctor keeps them separate. He believes that her ailment, psychic in origin, is due to guilt, and that she is therefore in need of a divine. He foresees her eventual suicide (l. 76).

Generally this scene shows that the womanly nature (as then understood) of Lady Macbeth has been violated.

ACT V, SCENE ii

Plot summary. The scene takes place in the country near Dunsinane. Menteith, Caithness, Angus, Lennox, and their soldiers enter. They are Scottish rebels, who have not left their native land, the "many worthy fellows that were out" of whom Ross had told Malcolm and Macduff in the previous act. Menteith reports that the English forces, led by Malcolm, his uncle Siward, and Macduff, are near. They are burning for revenge, and their righteous cause would raise the dead to do battle. Angus says that the native rebel army will meet the English near Birnam Wood. A short discussion follows as to who makes up the English army. Donalbain is not there, but Siward's son is there and many other young men. Menteith asks about Macbeth's situation. Caithness replies that Macbeth is strongly fortifying Dunsinane. Caithness continues, "Some say he's mad; others, that lesser hate him, / Do call it valiant fury: but, for certain, / He cannot buckle his distempered cause / Within the belt of rule." Angus says that Macbeth can no longer escape from his crimes: every minute ("Now minutely") "revolts upraid his faith-breach." His men obey him only by command. "Nothing in love. Now does he feel his title / Hang loose about him, like a giant's robe / Upon a dwarfish thief." Menteith adds in a rhetorical question that Macbeth cannot be blamed for being frightened "When all that is within him does condemn / Itself for being there." Caithness says that they will march ahead "To give obedience where 'tis truly owed." And it is agreed that they will pour out as much blood as is necessary for their country's cure.

Critical analysis. Scenes ii through the ending, which were originally continuous, are marked by intermittent drumming which has the effects of unifying this part of the play and of charging the somewhat prosaic character of Macduff as an instrument of Nemesis. A combined Scottish-English army, ardent for revenge and purging Scotland of Macbeth, is marching toward Birnam Wood. Lines 3–5 say that their heartfelt causes would rouse even a paralytic. Mention of Donalbain, certainly irrelevant to a modern audience, would presumably have been understood in earlier days: Donalbain, who succeeded Malcolm, had been brought up, according to Holinshed, in the old Celtic manners and desired to keep Scotland free from English influence whereas Malcolm was striving to unite the two kingdoms and was certainly susceptible to English manners and influences. *Hence Donalbain's absence*, ll. 12–16, prepares us for the desperate madness of Macbeth in the next scene—something which we have not seen before. Macbeth has evidently suffered military reverses, for, having previously been in the field, he is about to retire to a fortified castle, where he does not even command a loyal following. Caithness, Menteith, and Angus seem to think that Macbeth's conscience is bothering him; indeed, Angus at l. 18 says that everytime a follower revolts, this act reminds Macbeth of his own perfidy.

With regard to ll. 20–22, Spurgeon, analyzing clothes imagery, writes that a "small ignoble man encumbered and degraded by garments unsuited to him should be put against the view emphasized by some critics (notably Coleridge and Bradley) of the likeness between Macbeth and Milton's Satan in grandeur and sublimity." (Critics of Milton's *Paradise Lost* are accustomed to seeing many parallels between Macbeth and Satan.) Spurgeon concludes that Shakespeare sees Macbeth both as Bellona's bridegroom and as a dwarfish thief. Caithness at l. 18 speaks of Malcolm as "the med'cine of the sickly weal" with imagery that would have especially appealed to King James, who learned from his tutor, George Buchanan, author of *De Jure Regni apud Scotos*, to think of a king as the physician of the commonwealth, an image that James employed in his *Counter-Blaste to Tobacco* (1604).

ACT V, SCENE iii

Plot summary. The scene is in a room at Dunsinane. Macbeth, the doctor, and attendants enter. Macbeth wants to hear no more reports of men deserting him. He cannot fear, for the prophecy had been that no man born of woman will defeat him, and Malcolm has been born of woman. A servant, white-faced with fear, enters. The servant informs Macbeth that ten thousand soldiers of the English power are approaching. Macbeth keeps interrupting his servant's report with scornful remarks because the servant looks frightened and undoubtedly speaks in a frightened way. After the servant leaves, Macbeth speaks a soliloquy, which he twice interrupts with calls for his armor-bearer, Seyton. In the soliloquy he says that he is "sick at heart" when he sees . . . and we do not learn what makes him sick at heart, for he interrupts by crying once more for Seyton. Then he says that this attack "Will cheer me ever" or topple him from the throne now. He has lived long enough, he feels; ". . . my way of life / Is fall'n into the sere, the yellow leaf." All that one ordinarily expects of old age, such as "honor, love, obedience, troops of friends," Macbeth must not expect to have. Instead he will receive "Curses, not loud, but deep, mouth-honor, breath"; these who give the mouth-honor know in their hearts that they do not want to give it but dare not withhold it. Seyton enters and

Universitätsbuchhandlung Ziehank
6900 Heidelberg   Inh. W. Turk
Tel. 06221/10081-83

Quittung-Nr.: 14495/18   Datum 08.07.92

MONARCH N.518 *SHAKESPEARE:MACBETH
0671005162   1 /DM 14.90 /DM= 14.90

Netto   13.93 DM
7.00 % MWST   0.97 DM
Zu zahlender Betrag   14.90 DM

Gegeben: 14.90 DM

Betrag dankend bar erhalten

says that all reports (probably of the approaching English and of the desertions) are true. Macbeth says that he will fight until his "flesh is hacked" from his bones. Macbeth wishes Seyton to help him on with his armor. Seyton tells him that it is not necessary yet. Macbeth insists. He gives orders to send out men who will hang those who say they are frightened. He interrupts his talk and addresses the doctor, of whom he inquires about his wife. The doctor tells Macbeth that Lady Macbeth is not so much physically ill as she is bothered by illusions which come one after the other and keep her from sleep. "Cure her of that . . . ," Macbeth tells the doctor. He then asks the doctor whether the latter can help a person sick in his mind. The doctor replies that in that situation a person must help himself. "Throw physic [medicine] to the dogs . . . ," replies Macbeth. Macbeth, talking at once to the doctor and to Seyton, tells the latter to help him on with his armor, to send out . . . for something—the order is never completed . . . to take off his armor. To the doctor he says that his nobles are leaving him; and then he says that he would greatly applaud the doctor if the latter could find a cure for his sick country. Has the doctor heard that the English are coming? The doctor replies in the affirmative. But Macbeth is now back to Seyton, commanding him to follow Macbeth with the armor. Macbeth exits saying that he will not be frightened "Till Birnam forest come to Dunsinane."

Critical analysis. This scene exhibits a Macbeth not hitherto observed. He speaks for the first time in public that supernatural spirits have guaranteed him against defeat by any "man that's born of woman," and he applies the oracular saying to Malcolm. He raves against "false thanes," bidding them join "the English epicures." Shakespeare perhaps derived from Holinshed the idea that "fine fare" and "superfluous gormandizing" were brought into Scotland by the English. Following George Orwell and extending his thought, one may say that northerners in various countries tend to think of southerners as being stained with "epicurism" (Epicurus would be aghast at this use of his name), as well as softness, untruthfulness, lechery, and so forth.

A Servant enters whose appearance Macbeth does not like: he shouts at him "thou cream-faced loon." *Loon* is usually glossed "worthless fellow," but it may conceivably mean, as Weston Babcock thinks, the aquatic bird, a meaning probably current circa 1606 in spoken (though not written) English. Macbeth under the impetus of his anger goes from "cream-fac'd loon" to "goose look" to "lily-liver'd" to "linen-cheeks," all epithets reflecting badly on the Servant's manliness. The Servant bears the bad news of the approach of the English army. Macbeth shrieks, "Take thy face hence," an admirable expression because, like Lady Macduff's "What are these faces?" it presents a concentrated expression. One supposes that the Servant alarms Macbeth's following.

Seyton, the armour-bearer, enters. Macbeth calls three times for armour, and then says, "Pull't off, I say," his indecisiveness suggesting his insecurity. He knows that the English force arrayed against him amounts to "ten thousand," but he does not know how many revolted Scots have joined it. The memorably phrased speech in ll. 22–29 indicates lapse of time, contrasts Macbeth with Duncan, and shows that Macbeth not only wanted the crown but the peaceful possession of it.

Theory of humors. He turns to the Doctor with a question about Lady Macbeth's health, and he understands that his wife's condition is psychosomatic. So he bids the physician erase from her mind "a rooted sorrow," and "Cleanse the stuff'd bosom of that perilous stuff / Which weighs upon the heart." Physiologically any of the four humors—melancholy, blood, phlegm, and choler—burnt by the extreme heat accompanying passion, was called melancholy adust. This sediment or residue could not be absorbed by the body and tended to choke the veins. It was a cause of madness and would ultimately destroy life. Hence, Macbeth hopes that physical purgation, effected before it is too late, may conduce to the cure of mental illness. The Doctor evidently diagnoses Lady Macbeth's illness as mental in origin and asserts in effect that he does not undertake psychiatry.

In a masterly touch at l. 49 Macbeth tells the Doctor, "the thanes fly from me," a remark that suggests at once that Macbeth is under pressure dropping his guard and that physicians by their calling hear secrets. It is evident that Macbeth rests his security, such as it is, upon the prophecies regarding Birnam Wood and lack of fear for a man born of woman. The armed head, which might well jar him, has been cast out of mind.

ACT V, SCENE iv

Plot summary. The scene occurs in the country near Birnam Wood. With drum, colors, and soldiers marching, enter Malcolm, Siward, Siward's son, Macduff, Menteith, Caithness, Angus, Lennox, and Ross. Malcolm addresses the native rebels, saying that he hopes that soon bedrooms will be safe. (Duncan was murdered in a bedroom.) Menteith replies that his group does not doubt that at all. Siward asks for the name of the wood which they are near. He is told that it is Birnam Wood. Malcolm announces that every soldier is to cut off a bough from a tree so that the army may fool the enemy by camouflage. Siward says that "the confident tyrant" (Macbeth) remains in Dunsinane and will sit out his antagonists' siege in the palace. Malcolm adds that that strategy is Macbeth's principal hope for victory. For whenever Macbeth's soldiers have the opportunity to do so, they revolt against him. Macduff and Siward agree that they should not speculate on such matters; rather they should do their jobs as good soldiers, and time will tell whether or not their speculations are right. The group exits marching.

Critical analysis. This brief scene, based on Holinshed, exhibits the combined English-Scottish force marching toward Dunsinane, where Macbeth is on the point of incarcerating himself in his castle for his last stand. Malcolm, seeing Birnam Wood (Americans would say "Woods") before him, orders his force to cut boughs that would disguise their numbers as the army approaches Macbeth. It is important to note that *Malcolm is unaware that he is fulfilling Macbeth's vision of "a child crowned, with a tree in his hand."* It is equally important to observe that Malcolm is unaware that he is implementing the prophecy of the Witches to the effect that Macbeth is in no danger until Birnam Wood come to Dunsinane. Not coincidence but Providence overrules the action. The moving wood imparts the spectacle not of wild revenge but of order and even ceremony in league with nature advancing to restore kingly dignity to Scotland. John P. Cutts points out that George Sandys, in his commentary to *Ovid's Metamorphosis Englished, Mythologized, and Represented in Figures* . . . (1632), placed the moving of Birnam Wood toward Dunsinane in suggestive parallel with Orpheus' music calming the inebriated Bacchantes.

Malcolm dilates hopefully on the weak state of Macbeth's defensive forces, suggesting that some have revolted and that those who cannot revolt accordingly serve from constraint. In ll. 14–16 Macduff gracefully checks the young man: "Let our opinions, to be accurate, await the outcome, which will disclose the truth." Though confident of vanquishing Macbeth, Macduff is less sanguine and more experienced than Malcolm.

ACT V, SCENE v

Plot summary. The scene takes place within Dunsinane castle. Macbeth, Seyton, and Macbeth's soldiers enter with drum and colors. Macbeth cries out that he and his soldiers will remain in the castle because the castle's "strength / Will laugh a siege to scorn." He will be able to endure until his enemies are depleted by famine and illness. If his enemies were not reinforced with men who have deserted him, his army might have gone out and met the enemy and beaten them back.

A cry of women interrupts Macbeth. Seyton goes off to discover the cause. "I have almost forgot the taste of fears," says Macbeth aside. At one time, he continues, he would have had chills on hearing a cry in the night; and at a horrible story his hair would have stood on end. "I have supp'd full with horrors: Direness, familiar to my slaughterous thoughts, / Cannot once start me," he concludes. Seyton re-enters to tell Macbeth that Lady Macbeth is dead. "She should have died hereafter . . ." says Macbeth. *He then speaks one of the most famous Shakespearean speeches, which begins*, "Tomorrow, and tomorrow, and tomorrow . . . ." The main idea of this speech is that all the future and all the past have no significance. The speech ends with Macbeth's saying that life "is a tale / Told by an idiot, full of sound and fury, / Signifying nothing."

A Messenger enters and tells Macbeth of something that seems unbelievable: ". . . I looked toward Birnam, and anon, methought, / The wood began to move." Macbeth cries, "Liar, and slave!" The Messenger insists upon the truth of his statement. Macbeth says that if the Messenger is lying, the latter will hang on a tree alive. If the Messenger is telling the truth, Macbeth would be indifferent to the Messenger's hanging him. Macbeth says that he begins "To doubt the equivocation of the fiend, / That lies like truth." He had been told not to fear until Birnam Wood came to Dunsinane, "and now a wood / Comes toward Dunsinane." Macbeth gives the order to fight outside the castle, for if what the Messenger said be true, it does not matter whether or not his army outwait the siege in the castle or wait outside. "I 'gin to be aweary of the sun," reflects Macbeth, "And wish the estate o' the world were now undone." Then he cries, "Ring the alarm bell! Blow wind! come, wrack! / At least we'll die with harness on our back."

Critical analysis. This scene forwards the plot by reporting the death of Lady Macbeth and by informing Macbeth that Birnam Wood is moving toward Dunsinane. Macbeth shows apathy in learning of his wife's death, anger at hearing of Birnam Wood, and apathy again at the end of the scene.

When a cry of women arises offstage, Macbeth marvels at his present inability to register shock. "I have supp'd full with horrors," he says with a suggestion that as a devouring hell-kite he has surfeited upon innocent victims. Seyton the armor-bearer announces that the Queen is dead. Macbeth responds, "She should have died hereafter," meaning that she was bound to die at some time or other. This remark is not necessarily a reflection of callousness, although it may be: Romeo has almost nothing to say (V.i.24 ff.) when he learns of Juliet's death. There is a rumor that Lady Macbeth committed suicide (V.ix.36–37), but she may have died of a broken heart caused by the slaughter of Lady Macduff. An effect of having Lady Macbeth die before her husband is somewhat to soften the catastrophe: Macbeth becomes more sick at heart and attracts enough sympathy to permit one to view his approaching death as justice rather than to rejoice over it with personal hatred.

"Tomorrow, and Tomorrow . . ." Macbeth's speech "Tomorrow, and tomorrow, and tomorrow" has been finely interpreted by Fitzroy Pyle as imaging a funeral procession through a vault with each day being a mourner that carries a candle. Macbeth thinks of life as nothing but illusions and evanescence. Abruptly changing the imagery, as Shakespeare does in his mature manner, Macbeth in effect says in l. 21: "Events by syllables go on, one after another, until the last syllable has been registered; and time is merged with eternity." Conviction grows on Macbeth; and, dropping his interest in the burial vault, he concludes that both life and death are futile—"Out, out, brief candle!" This expression could mean that Macbeth believes in the death of the soul with the death of the body or, less probably, that trust in this life is but trust in a candle and a shadow. Dr. Johnson took the view that the speech broadly means that "life is such that instead of enjoying today we entertain hopes of tomorrow; and when tomorrow comes, then we hope for the next day. Days thus spent bring fools to the grave." Frye has interestingly assembled similar remarks from others, including John Donne, of Shakespeare's time. In this purple patch the word "poor" in "poor player" should be stressed because the pity of an actor is

that he leaves nothing behind him. But "struts and frets" shows contempt chiefly for life rather than for acting because an actor imitates life. Macbeth's despair penetrates us more through the power of the phrasing than from the terrible situation. Irving Ribner finely says: "As his link with humanity weakens, so also does his desire to live, until at last he sinks into total despair, the medieval sin of *Acedia*, which is the surest evidence of his damnation." In the coda of this speech Shakespeare should not be thought to be expressing his personal philosophy, for the fact is that we do not know what Shakespeare thought about anything except such elementary matters as that New Place, Stratford, was worth buying. We know this because his plays lack *raisonneurs*, authorial mouthpieces (except, possibly, Ulysses in *Troilus and Cressida*), and because there is a most plentiful absence of letters, diaries, and reported conversations to document the point that a given character in a given speech is voicing Shakespeare's own sentiments.

From Kemble to Kurosawa. A Messenger, entering, gives an eyewitness report that Birnam Wood seems to be moving to Dunsinane. In the Kurosawa filmed version, birds from Birnam Wood "fly desperately" through the castle of Dunsinane in reminiscence of the verses (III.iv.123–25) of choughs and magpies revealing "The secret'st man of blood." The Messenger slightly individualizes himself by standing up to Macbeth: "I should report that which I say I saw." Macbeth becomes abusive. The actor Philip Kemble found it necessary to argue that a stage direction "Striking him," placed after l. 34 in the acting version, is not found in the Folio. Certainly, however, Macbeth is at this point, as Kemble said, in a "bewilderment of fear and rage," even offering himself to be hanged if the report about Birnam Wood should prove to be correct. Again Macbeth, losing control, quotes the prophecy in public. When he says that he is growing "a-weary with the sun," the sun should be thought as symbolizing light, reason, reality, legitimate kingship, and Christ. The scene ends with a desperate couplet by no wise equal in poetic merit to the speech beginning "tomorrow, and tomorrow, and tomorrow."

ACT V, SCENE vi

Plot summary. The scene takes place on a plain before the castle. Enter Malcolm, Old Siward, Macduff, and their armies, with boughs. Malcolm says that they are now near enough (to the castle) to put down the branches of Birnam Wood, which they have been using as camouflage. Malcolm then makes the arrangements for battle. Macduff gives the order for the trumpets to sound, which announce the coming of "blood and death."

Critical analysis. In this brief scene Malcolm commands his army to throw down their "leavy screens," *one of the last reversals in the play.* The coming of Birnam Wood to Dunsinane, Holloway says, is "a vivid emblem . . . a dumbshow of nature overturning antinature." John Gerlach makes the same point: "When the forest moves in Act V, it is true enough that nature, rampaging beyond control since the murder of Duncan, is now through human bidding restoring order." *A company carrying green branches was a traditional part of Maying processions; so this spectacle would have seemed less unnatural to the first spectators than it does to us.*

Malcolm orders Old Siward to lead the assault on the castle.

ACT V, SCENE vii

Plot summary. The scene occurs on the field of battle. Macbeth enters. He feels like a bear tied to a stake in the spectator sport of bear-baiting. (In that game the bear is tied to a stake and dogs are sent out to fight him.) Macbeth then refers to the prophecy that is his last hope. He does not believe a man exists who was not born of woman. "Such a one / Am I to fear, or none," he says. Young Siward enters. When he asks Macbeth for the latter's name, Macbeth replies that Siward will be afraid to hear it. "No; though thou call'st thyself a hotter name / Than any is in hell," answers the young man. But on hearing Macbeth's name, Young Siward says, "The devil himself could not pronounce a title / More hateful to mine ear." Macbeth adds, "No, nor more fearful." But the remark only incites the young man to call Macbeth a liar and to start the fighting. Macbeth kills Young Siward, and this leads Macbeth to the grimly humorous conclusion that Siward was born of woman.

Macbeth leaves the stage. Macduff enters. Macduff has been looking for Macbeth. Macduff feels that if Macbeth dies without Macduff's having a part in killing him, he, Macduff, will be haunted by the ghosts of his family. He does not want to fight with the hired Irish foot-soldiers ("kerns"); he will either fight with Macbeth or not at all. He hears a great noise and believes that should denote the presence of a great person. He exits saying, "Let me find him, Fortune! / And more I beg not."

Macduff's exit is followed by the entrance of Old Siward and Malcolm. Perhaps because his son's body has been in one way or another removed from the stage; perhaps because the stage arrangement is such that the audience can see his dead son and he cannot, Siward is unaware that his son has been slain. He is telling Malcolm that the castle will surrender without much fight; that Macbeth's men fight on Macbeth's enemy's side as well as on Macbeth's. Malcolm almost has the victory clinched, says Siward. They exeunt as Siward shows Malcolm into the castle.

Critical analysis. When Macbeth exclaims that he is now tied like a bear to a stake, the image reduces him to that which he in some respects is, an animal. Polanski's filmed version made the bear-image come alive by having staged a bear-baiting episode as entertainment during the banquet scene: the bear, bloodied and then killed, foreshadows the death of the tyrant, and the remark in V.vii is therefore a flashback. The fact is, however, that Macbeth is not now in his castle but near it.

After an unpleasant exchange with Young Siward, marked by

the mutual "thou," Macbeth kills the young man. It must be so because, as the eighteenth-century critic Steevens remarked, "Shakespeare designed Macbeth should appear invincible till he encountered the object destined for his destruction."

Macduff, entering, declares that he will kill no one but Macbeth. In his soliloquy the word "kerns" indicates that Macbeth is depending upon Irish mercenaries as Macdonwald the rebel did before him.

Malcolm and Old Siward, the latter of whom unaccountably fails to spot his son's corpse, enter the castle with conversation suggesting the ease with which it will be taken. Malcolm says, "We have met with foes / That strike beside us," which could mean that they "deliberately miss us."

ACT V, SCENE viii

Plot summary. The scene occurs in another part of the field of battle. Macbeth enters and says that he will not behave like the Roman soldier who would commit suicide before he allowed himself to be captured and killed by his enemies (like Brutus or Antony in other plays of Shakespeare). As long as Macbeth sees others alive, he would rather give others wounds than himself. Macduff enters and cries, "Turn, hell-hound, turn!" Macbeth tells his pursuer that he has been avoiding Macduff more than he has avoided any other man, for "my soul is too much charged / With blood of thine already." He tells Macduff not to fight him. But as an answer Macduff does little more than show his sword ready for battle. In the midst of the fight Macbeth warns Macduff that the latter is wasting time fighting, for Macbeth leads "a charmed life" and cannot be defeated by "one of woman born." Macduff tells his adversary to give up hope, because "Macduff was from his mother's womb / Untimely ripped." Macbeth cries, "Accursed be that tongue . . . ," for it frightens him. Macbeth continues, "And be these juggling fiends no more believed, / That palter with us in a double sense; / That keep the word of promise to our ear, / And break it to our hope." Macbeth refuses to fight with Macduff. In that case, Macduff says, Macbeth must surrender and must submit to being displayed as a monstrous rarity in the side show. Macbeth refuses to surrender. He will neither serve Malcolm nor "be baited with the rabble's curse." Despite the fact that the conditions of his defeat as foretold in the prophecies have arrived, he will fight to the end. Placing his shield before him, Macbeth challenges Macduff, "... lay on, Macduff; / And damned be him that first cries, 'Hold, enough!'"

Critical analysis. The outcome of this battle scene is never in doubt. Macbeth considers suicide after defeat, connecting this course (as Cleopatra does in *Antony and Cleopatra*) with Roman practice; he rejects it.

Macduff, entering and encountering Macbeth *vis-à-vis*, prepares for the moment of prophetic truth in the sense of the Witches and in the larger sense of the Bible that "all they that take the sword, shall perish with the sword" (Matt. 26,52). *Lines 4–6 are the closest to repentance ever seen in the characterization of Macbeth. Macbeth intellectually understands that he has erred, and in some degree he regrets his error; but he does not repent in the Christian sense.* When Macduff assures him that he is a servant of Satan, he does not even try to gloss over his wickedness with a conventional religiosity. Yet Macbeth's fear of Macduff is chiefly spiritual rather than physical; it is like his fear of Banquo but stronger in degree. Because of prophecy and tenderheartedness, Macbeth wishes to avoid a fight with Macduff, and he does so by informing Macduff of the prophecy to the effect that no man born of woman shall conquer him. Macduff then acquaints Macbeth with his Caesarian birth. *The prophecy of the bloody child, quite unknown to Macduff as Macduff's Caesarian birth is to Macbeth, is fulfilled by an overruling Providence.* Macbeth curses the Witches for their equivocations and declares that he will not fight Macduff. Then Macduff offers Macbeth the option of living out his life in captivity like an animal in a zoo, *a speech not out of character for Macduff but one that is unexpected*. Macbeth should accept this offer if he wishes to repent, but his pride is recrudescent. Like Cleopatra, he cannot bear to present himself abjectly before the jeering rabble. So he fights and dies. Kean, a famous Macbeth in the nineteenth century, is reported by Hazlitt as falling "at last finely, with his face downwards, as if to cover the shame of his defeat." Kean crawled for his sword, and "died" as he touched it. Polanski's death of an excessively villainized Macbeth, by reason of its emphasis on bloodshed, tends to debase tragedy into melodrama.

Differences over staging of Macbeth's death. The action at the ending of this scene is a problem. If one inspects the Variorum edition, he finds that early critics thought Macbeth to have been killed onstage, his body then being dragged offstage, decapitated, and the head brought back on. Davenant, the Restoration "improver" of *Macbeth*, and Garrick brought no head back but rather Macbeth's sword. In the twentieth century, the severed head is sometimes returned (certainly it is in Polanski's gory version) and sometimes not; producers evidently feel awkwardness here. The important point is the identity of the First Apparition: is it Macduff, as most commentators think, or is it Macbeth, as in Hardin Craig's opinion and as in Sir Laurence Olivier's stage version at Stratford, England in 1954? A secondary point, suggesting the soundness of the latter view, is the final reminiscence of Saul in the characterization of Macbeth. W. B. Hunter, Jr., argues that the death of Macbeth occurs "in such a way that the victim can be killed in full view or hidden. The play, that is, can be performed in accordance with the classical principle of decorum, or it can be acted with sufficient blood and guts to satisfy an average Jacobean playgoer." *Thus, King James could be soothed by a decorous play and by one in which he, the chief intended victim of the Gunpowder Plot, would not have to witness the staged killing of a king.*

ACT V, SCENE ix

Plot summary. The scene occurs within the castle. Malcolm, Old Siward, Ross, and their army enter victoriously. Malcolm says that he wishes that friends who are not present were safely here (that is, not dead). Old Siward replies that (in war) some must die. Yet, from all he can tell, the great victory of this day was achieved at the expense of few lives. Malcolm says that Macduff and Old Siward's son are missing. Ross tell Old Siward that Young Siward "paid a soldier's debt." That is, he died as a man should. After Old Siward is assured that his son had indeed died as a man should and had wounds on his face before he died, the father says, "Why then, God's soldier be he!" If Old Siward had as many sons as he has hairs on his head, he would not wish them better deaths than this one. Malcolm says that he will give the young man more grief than his father has given, for the young man deserves it; but Old Siward insists otherwise: "They say he parted well and paid his score: / And so, God be with him!" (The idea in "paid his score" is that each man owes God a life, and we pay God our debt when we die.)

Macduff now enters carrying Macbeth's head. He hails Malcolm as king, points to Macbeth's head, and announces that now "the time is free." He then asks the nobility (the "kingdom's pearl") to shout with him, "Hail, King of Scotland!" This the nobility does. Malcolm says that he will not permit a long time to pass before he pays his debt to those present. The thanes shall become earls, the first earls ever named in Scotland. Whatever else remains to be done, "which would be planted newly with the time," such necessities as recalling Scotland's exiles, finding out the agents of the cruel Macbeth and his "fiend-like queen," who, it is thought, committed suicide—such necessities, Malcolm says, he "will perform in measure, time, and place." Giving thanks to all and inviting them to his coronation, Malcolm leads the actors off the stage in their final exeunt.

Critical analysis. Old Siward, receiving news of his son's death, is reassured that the young man has perished in soldierly fashion because his wounds were "on the front." Old Siward appears an ideal soldier: having taken Macbeth's castle, he promptly turns it over to Malcolm and recognizes him as master. Indeed, the characterization of Old Siward, a Dane, may be thought a compliment to Christian, King of Denmark, who with his brother-in-law, James I of England, witnessed the first performance of *Macbeth* at Hampton Court in 1606.

Then the Folio (there was no Quarto) reads, "Enter Macduffe; with Macbeths head." The source is Holinshed's *Chronicles*: "Then cutting his head from his shoulders, he set it vpon a pole, and brought it vnto Malcolme." Malone inserted the stage-direction "on a pole." The textual evidence for the pole is found in ll. 20–21: "Behold where stands / Th' usurper's cursed head." Macbeth's head is not dragged in by the hair nor is it resting in someone's arms. Julian Mates emphasizes the point that Londoners were familiar with the practice of placing traitors' heads on poles atop the southern gate towers of London Bridge; so the first audiences could easily see not only the fulfillment of the Witches' prophecy of the armed head but also the association with treachery. Macduff, in short, has dragged Macbeth's corpse to decapitate it offstage and impale the head; then he re-enters with the poled head, plants it, and speaks in felicitation of Malcolm as King of Scotland. ". . . the time is free," says Macduff.

Barbara Parker points out that the play's ending sees the restoration of natural time, *e.g.*, that associated with planting and harvesting, as distinguished from that time which sees "the future in the instant." Macduff continues, "I see thee compass'd with thy kingdom's pearl," which Paul explains as the dependent fiefs of the imperial diadem placed or to be placed on Malcolm's head; the primary reference is of course to the crown. *In his filmed version*, Polanski here emphasizes the crown on Malcolm's head, not wanting us to forget that it was for this crown that Macbeth did murder; and he even goes beyond the text to show Donalbain, at the conclusion of the play, riding to the cave of the Witches, and thus suggesting that another Macbeth is in the making. Another extra-textual touch that has been used (not by Polanski) is keeping the Witches aloft during the last scene so that they can join in the concluding cry, "Hail, King of Scotland!" If this insertion is made, the Witches become a mute chorus of Fates and assume a prominence that Shakespeare never intended. "Hail" here, unlike its earlier application to Macbeth, unites ceremony with substance.

The last speech: restoration of order. Malcolm, here as earlier, shows the man submerged in the ruler. Exhibiting neither self-glorification nor condescension, he undertakes himself and magnifies his thanes with the title of "earls." He promises to call home Scottish exiles who fled Macbeth. Malcolm is known in Scottish history as Malcolm Canmore, who with Saint Margaret the English princess, founded on April 25, 1057, his coronation day, the first dynastic succession that Scotland ever had. Because Shakespeare does not wish Macbeth to have any excuse for his deed (there is, however, the matter of the royal slip seen in I.iii.104), he obscures Malcolm's innovation of hereditary monarchy and suppression of tanist law (*i.e.*, the idea that the monarchy was elective within the descendants of Macalpine). The hereditary principle is apotheosized in the cauldron scene, which must have pleased James immensely with its depiction of eight sovereigns in lineal descent one from the other. *So the play ends with the last speech being assigned Malcolm rather than Macduff in observance of the tragic convention that the highest-ranking character left alive is to speak last, thus showing the restoration of order after the tempest.* It might be remarked that although Shakespeare is here following a pattern of tragedy, the ending of *Macbeth* is in the atmosphere of his chronicle and history plays.

CHARACTER ANALYSES

Macbeth

When we first hear of Macbeth, he is a man much honored by his countrymen for his leading and courageous part in defense of his good king and native land. However, almost as soon as we meet him, we realize that he is both ambitious and murderous. For as soon as the Witches greet him with the title of future king, Macbeth thinks of murdering Duncan, the current king. But Macbeth is not merely the kind of man who serves his king until he has an opportunity of killing the king. Macbeth, though he may wish to murder Duncan for Duncan's crown, nevertheless also wishes to be a good man. In fact he thinks of himself basically as a good man. This becomes obvious from his fright and his consciousness of his fright that result when he pictures himself murdering Duncan. Nevertheless, the powerful drive of his ambition has dangerously affected him. Macbeth regards the predictions not so much as predictions but as "supernatural soliciting," that is, as requests to him from powers greater than man to attain his goal of the crown. Since Macbeth has mainly homicidal methods in mind, he in effect thinks of the predictions as invitations to murder. Although Macbeth does not understand the trick his mind has played on him, he has in fact been warned away from falling into the very trap laid for him by his ambitions and by the Witches. Banquo warns Macbeth, after the latter has learned that he has been made the Thane of Cawdor, that the agents of the devil sometimes tell us small truths "to betray's / In deepest consequence." But the unheeding Macbeth in the very next speech refers to the predictions as "supernatural soliciting."

Now, Macbeth's conscience must contend not only with his powerful ambitions. Macbeth's conscience must also contend with Lady Macbeth, his wife, and Macbeth's love for his wife. Macbeth's love for his wife is so great that his ambitions strive as much for her as for himself. In his letter to her telling of his meeting with the Witches he calls her "my dearest partner of greatness" and he says that he wishes her not to be ignorant of what greatness "is promis'd *thee*." All of his thoughts, when he thinks of the pleasures and prestige of the kingship, include his wife. She on her part loves him equally and wishes to see him king at least as much as she wishes to see herself queen. But she is aware of his prickly conscience, which would make it difficult for him "To catch the nearest way," that is, the murderous way. She therefore uses the most effective method at her command, shame. Macbeth, after all, is a soldier, and he loves his wife. Neither for himself as a soldier nor before his wife would Macbeth want to appear as a coward. So despite his decision not to go ahead with the murder, when Lady Macbeth accuses her husband of cowardice in making his decision, he succumbs to her, and they continue with their plans for the crime.

Why had Macbeth decided against committing violence for the kingship? In a soliloquy in the seventh scene of the first act, he tells us that it is not death in the next world that he fears. Rather, he is afraid that his crime for the kingship will teach others to commit similar crimes when he is king. However, despite Macbeth's apparent indifference to religion and morality, he is really very much involved with both. He gives as further reason against killing Duncan the fact that Duncan is Macbeth's relative and his guest, both of which relationships urge Macbeth against committing the crime. And a final reason for not killing Duncan is that pity should prevent Macbeth from harming the good man and gentle king that Duncan has been. For most Elizabethans these reasons would have implied a concern with religion and morality, the extent of which Macbeth does not consciously admit.

Macbeth's internal conflict. Yet Macbeth allows himself to be shamed into the crime by Lady Macbeth. But, while she has whipped him into committing the act, she has not succeeded in silencing his conscience or stopping his concern with eternal things. After the murder he is distressed that he has not been able to say "Amen" at the end of prayers he had heard two men reciting. And at the same time his conscience hurts so, that he thinks he hears voices which cry, "Sleep no more! / Macbeth does murder sleep. . . ." He is in fact so hampered in his actions by the conflict between his knowledge that he has committed the crime and his abhorrence of it, that he becomes immobile. After the murder, when the two realize that Macbeth has brought the daggers from the murder chamber, Macbeth cannot return, even though returning means the difference between discovery and success. When Lady Macbeth has returned from placing the daggers near Duncan's attendants and hears the knocking at the gate, she almost has to push Macbeth into their bedroom so that they will look as though they have just been awakened.

The efforts of Macbeth and Lady Macbeth to attain the crown are successful. But Macbeth's awareness that he has given up his eternal soul makes him especially sensitive to his desire to make his kingship secure. Also contributing to his sensitivity is the fear that his crime may be discovered. The two motives make him first turn on Banquo and Fleance, Banquo's son, as the cause of his anxiety. Banquo was present at the Witches' meeting with Macbeth and that fact may make him especially able to discover Macbeth's crime. Also the Witches had predicted that Banquo's children rather than Macbeth's children would be kings. Perhaps Macbeth projects onto Banquo his own turn of thought and presumes that Banquo will attempt to attain the crown just as Macbeth himself had done so. Macbeth says, ". . . to that dauntless temper of his mind, / He [Banquo] hath a wisdom that doth guide his valor / To act in safety." At any rate, even if Banquo himself does not make an attempt, Macbeth's children will not succeed Macbeth and Banquo's will. In that case Macbeth will have lost not only his soul but the fruit of his labor in this world as well. For a man does not work only for his immediate profit in this world but also for the benefit of his children, who will make his name live on in honor. Macbeth therefore decides to have Banquo and Fleance killed.

Although, after the murder of Duncan, Macbeth's conscience had brought him nearly to immobility, he still decides to murder Banquo and Fleance. Nothing must stop him from living securely: "But let the frame of things disjoint, both the worlds suffer, / Ere we will eat our meal in fear, and sleep / In the affliction of these terrible dreams, / That shake us nightly." Despite these desperately resolute words his conscience is still able to attack him. At his state dinner the sight of Banquo's ghost makes him shake with guilt and fear. But this terrible experience causes Macbeth to be only more desperate in his efforts to repress his conscience and stem his fear and guilt. He will return to "the weird sisters," the Witches, whom he now recognizes as evil, so that he may "know / By the worst means, the worst." He repeats his determination that nothing shall stop him in his quest for security. "For mine own good / All causes shall give way . . . ." And all "Strange things" that he thinks of will immediately be acted out. Macbeth has completely committed himself to evil.

Macbeth's confusion of values. Why has Macbeth done this? Why has not the terrifying experience with Banquo's ghost warned him into repentance? Macbeth partially answers that question for us. "I am in blood / Stepped so far," he says, "that, should I wade no more, / Returning were as tedious as go o'er." Macbeth says that he finds it too tiresome to repent. But to someone who understands the worth of repentance, the process of repentance, hard as it may be, is hardly too tiresome. What has happened is that in making his first decision for evil instead of good and in accustoming himself to the thoughts necessary to maintain the results of that decision, Macbeth has confused the values of good and evil. That is, he has confused fair and foul, which confusion has all along been the devil's aim. Macbeth, in other words, has forgotten the comfort of a life without a screaming conscience or desperate thoughts. But behind his forgetfulness, at the very heart of his confusion of fair and foul, lies Macbeth's egotism. In order to repent, Macbeth would have to give up the kingship, which is giving him so much trouble. But he is unable to do so. The kingship still means more to him than quiet days and the possibility of heaven. Macbeth would rather rule in the hell he has made of his world than serve a good king and God in heaven. He therefore accustoms himself to his current life of anxiety, forgets the pleasures of easeful days, and finds it "tedious" to repent.

The irony of egotism. This same egotism is in evidence when Macbeth says that nothing will stand in the way of his security. "For mine own good, / All causes shall give way," he says. Earlier he had said that he would "let the frame of this disjoint" before he would live insecurely. Macbeth would destroy the world to gain security in his kingship. Of course, this is the reduction to absurdity which results from completely egotistic thought. Here is a man who would rule the world, yet would destroy it if he could not rule it securely. What world would there then be left to rule? And this foreshadows his later feeling, that he wishes the end of the world would come with his own desperate end. We see the irony of the completely egotistic pursuit. At the beginning of the play Macbeth had a good deal of stature. But his attempts at self-aggrandizement have reduced Macbeth to the size of a small man ineffectively flailing at a large world completely beyond his control. Really knowing this, Macbeth finds it "tedious" not only to repent but also to "go o'er," that is, to go on in his life.

However, he is not yet ready to admit the implication of this remark, which tells us that Macbeth despairs of this life as well as of the next. *And in fact he never does completely despair. No matter how much he comes to hate himself and life, his egotism also prevents him from ever simply surrendering his life.* He therefore works harder and harder to maintain his security. Banquo, his first object of fear, is now dead. But Macbeth is now frightened of Macduff and attempts to kill him. When Macduff escapes, Macbeth capriciously murders Macduff's family. Soon we hear that all of Scotland is frightened of Macbeth. The only way in which Macbeth can cause people to obey him is through fear, for that is the only motive for obedience that Macbeth can understand. *Macbeth has therefore turned Scotland into a reflection of his own mind; he has turned Scotland into hell.* But only devils and Macbeth wish to live in hell. And so his people begin to revolt against him. Macbeth becomes increasingly isolated. Not only are the people within Scotland revolting against him; Scotsmen have fled the land, and they are returning with an army of Englishmen to fight Macbeth. Finally, Macbeth is also isolated from the one person outside himself whom he has loved and for whom he has acted, his wife. She, too, had begun suffering the torments of a guilty conscience. Mainly because he loved her, he stopped telling her about his dire deeds so that she would not have them on her conscience. But she has felt responsibility for them as well as for those she actively helped to commit, and her conscience has increasingly paralyzed her mind. Macbeth, partially because he loved his wife and acting therefore more and more on his own, partially because her own conscience caused a mental breakdown, and finally because his wife dies, finds himself toward the end of the play in total isolation.

Macbeth's implied self-hatred. Thus isolated at the end of the play, Macbeth's final hope is the second set of prophecies of the Witches. They had told him that he would be harmed by no man born of woman and that he would not be defeated until Birnam Wood came to Dunsinane. Macbeth, thoroughly committed to evil and careless in his desperate search for assurance, believed them, although he should have realized from past experience that their promises of hope look good only on the surface. Now that he is isolated, the impossibility of his defeat, which the Witches' prophecies seemed to indicate, seems incredible. Yet Macbeth hopes on. But he only hopes; he barely believes. He is in a fever of anxious activity. He commands his servant to dress him in his armor; then he commands his servant to take it off.

But one decision seems firm. He will stay in the castle of Dunsinane, which is easily defended against a siege, and starve his enemies into defeat. But this resolution holds only until he sees Birnam Wood. It seems, he says, as though the Witches were only fooling with him. His desperation grows, and feeling the imminence of defeat, he orders what remains of his army out into the field, for he wishes to die at least actively fighting. But he also says that he is beginning to wish himself dead. Such a wish is not surprising. For when Macbeth wished earlier to see the destruction of the world if he should not be secure, when he found life too tedious to continue, when he felt anxious with guilt and fear, implied always was a hatred for himself and for life. And now in his final, desperate straits he expresses the hatred overtly.

And so Macbeth goes out into the field. Like a bear tied to a stake, he "must fight the course." He has one last hope, that his life "must not yield / To one of woman born." But finally he meets Macduff, who was "from his mother's womb / Untimely ripped." On hearing this bit of information Macbeth does not wish to fight with Macduff. But when Macduff threatens to make him a public show, Macbeth fights. He would rather die than bend to Malcolm or "be baited with the rabble's curse." Macbeth dies, then, not wholly to be scorned. His terrific egotism prevents him from bowing, as he should bow, before the rightful king, Malcolm. But it also prevents him from submitting to the indignity of being "baited with the rabble's curse." Although that indignity would present him as the monster he has become, Macbeth still thinks of himself as a man, and as such would rather die than suffer the indignity. This feeling in him reminds us of the worthy Macbeth at the beginning of the play. We also see that he still has the courage to act on his convictions, desperate though that courage may be. And it is not merely an animal courage. For he knows now that he must die. He fights as a man. *At the conclusion of the play, although we have come to abhor Macbeth, we cannot help but feel a certain admiration for him. But much more we have a sense of irony and waste: irony because some sterling qualities*

*have been put to such evil use, waste because Macbeth was a
potentially great man who was lost.*

**(See also the sections on Macbeth in "Intro-
duction to *Macbeth*," pp. 10–22.)**

Lady Macbeth

Lady Macbeth resembles her husband in a number of ways: she
honorably and efficiently carries out her duties as a member of
the aristocracy; she has powerful ambitions; she loves her
spouse and is ambitious at least as much for him as for herself;
finally, she also has a strong conscience. The main difference
between Lady Macbeth and Macbeth lies in Lady Macbeth's
utter refusal to listen to her conscience at the beginning of the
play. Actually, we never actually see a conflict in Lady Macbeth
between the good and evil parts of her as we do see in Macbeth.
We infer her conscience from the strength of her invocation to
the "spirits / That tend on mortal thoughts." She needs so strong
and so horrifying an invocation in order to repress an active
conscience. Knowing that her conscience would pain her for
planning and committing a murder, she calls on the spirits to
"Stop up the access and passage to remorse," to "take my milk
for gall," and not to permit heaven (another way of referring to
her conscience) "To cry, 'Hold, hold!'" Perhaps Lady Macbeth
finds it somewhat easier to ignore her conscience than her
husband can ignore his because her imagination is less vivid
than his. When he thinks of murdering Duncan, the picture of his
doing so appears before his eyes blotting out his real surroundings. Macbeth also sees daggers pointing him to the murder and
hears voices which cry, "Macbeth does murder sleep." Lady
Macbeth does not have the problem of contending with this kind
of imagination.

There is another difference between Lady Macbeth and Macbeth:
it is in their attitude toward each other. *Macbeth never in the
play thinks of manipulating his wife.* Later in the play, in order
to save her from the torments of her conscience, he does not tell

her of his plans for murder, but that is different from handling someone in such a way as to induce him to do something he may not want to do. *But Lady Macbeth does manipulate her husband.* This is not to say that she does not love him; on the contrary, her care for him and her tenderness toward him show that she does. She believes that her manipulating him into the murder of Duncan will attain for him the crown, which will eventually make him happier than his conscience will allow him to know that he will be. She therefore decides that she will "chastise [him] with the valor of [her] tongue." When the time comes for the fatal decision, she plays upon his manhood and his love for her. *Lady Macbeth is going to get her husband what he really wants, whether or not he knows he wants it.* Love, such as Lady Macbeth's which induces its object to try for more than its object wholly wants, is, we must conclude, influenced by egotism.

Now, when Lady Macbeth made the gigantic effort to repress her conscience, she apparently felt a necessity to do so only for the period in which the murder was to be committed. She never talks of needing the repression later. It appears as though she felt that once the murder was committed and "sovereign sway and masterdom" was attained, her guilt would be assuaged. Or, perhaps she felt that her conscience, once repressed by this great effort, would stay repressed. At any rate she counted neither on an irrepressible conscience nor on the consequences brought about by a kingship attained through violence, which consequences only brought on further acts of violence, which in turn only strengthened the conscience. The energy Lady Macbeth required to push down her conscience in the first place was great. She would need an ever-increasing energy to repress it, especially when it was always increasing in strength. Expecting only "sovereign sway and masterdom" without increased activity of her conscience, having consumed a tremendous amount of energy in first repressing her conscience, Lady Macbeth finally succumbs to its torments and can escape from them only in madness and suicide.

Her conscience victorious. The line of her deterioration can be traced in the play. In the first place she is not altogether successful in pushing down her conscience even for the period of the murder. She would herself have murdered Duncan "had he not resembled / My father as he slept," a resemblance probably made vivid by her conscience. After the murder, when Macbeth is making excuses for having murdered outright Duncan's attendants, Lady Macbeth faints. This may be a clever ruse on Lady Macbeth's part to take attention away from Macbeth, who seems to be talking too much. It may also be relief from the nervous tension engendered by her great efforts of the last few hours. However, these are just foreshadowings of what is in store for her. The next time we see her alone, she voices her sense of insecurity, "'Tis safer to be that which we destroy, / Than by destruction dwell in doubtful joy." And later in that same scene Macbeth speaks of these terrible dreams "That shake us nightly." The *us* refers to him and Lady Macbeth. However, she still retains enough energy to attempt to keep Macbeth from revealing his fears in the banquet scene. *Yet, once the guests have left in disorder, she is listless, all energy gone. She can speak only in single sentences*; Macbeth is dominant; he makes all the decisions, she none. *When next we see her, her conscience has emerged victorious.* Despite "the dignity of the whole body," which she apparently can maintain during the day and perhaps even in sleepwalking, *at night her conscience rips her with fears and shattered memories of crimes.* Worst of all, the stain and smell of Duncan's blood seems to cling to her hands. When we finally hear of her, it is thought that she has committed suicide. Almost certainly she has. We had heard earlier of her escape into madness, which was probably no escape, for undoubtedly the memories remained; and now suicide has become a final escape. Suicide was the only way in which she could control the conscience she so thoughtlessly and resolutely believed she could repress.

(See also the section on Lady Macbeth in "Introduction to *Macbeth*," pp. 10–22.)

Banquo

Banquo's function in the play is mainly as a foil to Macbeth. With Macbeth he is co-leader of Duncan's army against the rebel Macdonwald and the king of Norway. Like Macbeth he is an important member of the aristocracy, and he, too, meets the Witches who make prophecies concerning him. *Macbeth and he therefore have enough in common to make their different reactions and responses to events important.* We may first notice their different reactions to the Witches' prophecies. Macbeth regards them as "supernatural soliciting." But it is Banquo who reminds us that the devil tries to "Win us with honest trifles, to betray's / In deepest consequence." And Banquo's caution is the proper response, not Macbeth's egotistic assumption of "supernatural soliciting." Second, we may notice the images of time and growth so frequently used by Banquo, which indicate his acceptance of God's order and which contrast with Macbeth's attempt to control time for his own purposes. Listen to Banquo: "If you can look into the seeds of time, / And say which grain will grow and which will not . . ." (I.iii); "There if I grow, / The harvest is your own (I.iv); " . . . no jutty, frieze, / Buttress, nor coign of vantage, but this bird / Hath made his pendent bed, and procreant cradle . . ." (I.vi); " . . . our time does call upon's" (III.i). And those are samplings. Third, Banquo is wary not only of supernatural temptation but also of human temptation. Macbeth falls not only for the lure of the Witches but also for the temptation offered by his wife. But when Macbeth says to Banquo, "If you shall cleave to my consent, when 'tis, / It shall make honor for you," Banquo indicates in his reply that he will be involved in no dirty work for worldly gain: "So I lose none [honor] / In seeking to augment it [honor]. . . ."

More than a foil. But while Banquo in large part serves in the play as a foil to Macbeth, he, unlike most of the other supporting characters, interests us in and of himself. For Banquo is ambitious, and the ambition pulls strongly on him. Although he is cautious of the temptation Macbeth may warily have put to him, he *is*, after all, willing to confer with Macbeth about augmenting his honor—as long as no dirty work is afoot. Banquo strongly wishes to rise, but he wishes to do so without foul play. And his wish for worldly gain is so strong that, though he is not consciously tempted, he may have been unconsciously tempted. At the beginning of Act II he says to Macbeth, "I dreamt last night of the three weird sisters: / To you they have showed some truth." What did he dream about? Was it of a foul way of gaining his ambition? He had said earlier in the scene that he had had "cursed thoughts" in his sleep. His dreams, at any rate, show his powerful interest in what the Witches had forecast for him. Finally, although his soliloquy in Act III, Scene i, begins with a consideration of how Macbeth had attained the kingship, Banquo does not dwell on that subject long. Macbeth's acquisition of the crown only leads him to the thought of the truth of the Witches' prophecy to Macbeth and therefore to the possibility that their prophecy to him may also end in truth. But these revelations of Banquo's ambitious drives, while they make him more interesting to us in that they show him to be a man of conflicting motives, also accentuate his function as a foil to Macbeth. For like Macbeth, he is powerfully driven to worldly goals; but unlike Macbeth, he never confuses fair and foul. Also, no actor playing Banquo should forget what Macbeth says about him, for such an actor must show it in his bearing and in his pantomime. Banquo, says Macbeth, has a "dauntless temper of . . . mind" and a "wisdom that doth guide his valor / To act in safety." That is, Banquo is brave both physically and spiritually, and he has an intelligence that teaches his bravery to act with discretion.

Macduff

We first distinguish Macduff from the other members of the supporting cast when with Lennox he knocks at the gate after the murder of Duncan. The knocking itself is like the hammer-blow of fate, which Macbeth has called down upon himself by having committed the murder. Macduff is the instrument of that fate. This idea begins to emerge as Macduff is distinguished from

Lennox because the former enters Duncan's chamber to rouse Duncan only to discover Duncan dead. It is then Macduff who returns shouting horror at the fact of Duncan's murder. It is also Macduff who asks Macbeth why the latter has killed Duncan's attendants. Macduff is further impressed upon our consciousness when we learn of his decision against attending Macbeth's coronation. In discussing the coronation with Lennox, Macduff's ironic tone indicates his suspicion of Macbeth: "Well, may you see things well done there. . . ." Thus, with his few brief appearances and few lines Macduff has become rather important to us. While we cannot as yet understand *the full significance of Macduff as one of the knockers at the gate, we do recognize early in the play a basic antagonism between him and Macbeth, an antagonism that begins earlier than that of any other character in the play.*

Why Macduff leaves his family. Whether Macduff has attempted to encourage in others his own distrust of Macbeth, or whether he merely voiced his distrust, or whether he did neither of these, we do not know. We do know that his distrust of Macbeth was great enough for him to refuse a command to appear before Macbeth. The refusal, of course, makes for an untenable situation and Macduff understandably flees Scotland leaving his wife and children. Lady Macduff perhaps half believes her husband to be a traitor. A man who is not a traitor, she says, would not leave his family to a tyrant from whom he himself is running away. But in her distress and confusion Lady Macduff misses the intention of her husband's action. He has left Scotland without word to his family because he did not wish the family to be implicated. Macduff regarded Macbeth as a tyrant but not a mindless murderer of those who were completely innocent. By not warning his family of his flight, Macduff thought to free them of the possibility of any blame. The family would then live comfortably in its home and not become exiles in England. *This is the only construction that can be placed on Macduff's actions, for Macduff is neither coward, traitor, nor fool. But even Macduff could not see the depths to which Macbeth would sink.*

Symbolic avenger. Until the point at which his family is murdered, Macduff symbolizes the opposition to Macbeth that comes from the good man interested in the welfare of his country. But in England, when Macduff hears of the slaughter of his family, his role changes. He becomes the *determined avenger, symbolic* of those set upon the destruction of Macbeth because they are personally involved. *We can now see why Macduff as the instrument of fate knocked at the gate.* Macbeth, having fatefully murdered Duncan, inevitably ended in murdering innocent women and children. The inevitable avenger, therefore, is Macduff, symbolic of the husbands and fathers of the slaughtered innocents. Macbeth then, in killing Duncan, assured the course for the rest of his life and thus sealed his own doom. His doom is Macduff, for that purpose by fate "from his mother's womb / Untimely ripp'd." That is, Macbeth in killing Duncan in effect made sure that eventually a Macduff would kill Macbeth.

Duncan

Duncan is the good king under whom apparently a kingdom flourishes. In his soliloquy in Act I, Scene vii, Macbeth attests to Duncan's virtue and to Duncan's restrained usage of his kingly powers. When Duncan arrives at Macbeth's castle, Inverness, in the brief respite between the outrages perpetrated by Macdonwald and Macbeth, the descriptions of the atmosphere about Inverness given by Duncan and Banquo suggest the healthy, peaceful condition of the land during the rule by such a man as Duncan. That Duncan is aware of "no art / To find the mind's construction in the face" is not a criticism of Duncan. There is, in fact, no art which will do so. Only time will reveal the "mind's construction." The only early antagonist of Macbeth is Macduff, and he may have been suspicious of Macbeth only because he happened to ask Macbeth why the latter had killed Duncan's grooms and therefore may have been keenly watching Macbeth flounder in the reply. Antagonism to Macbeth grows as time reveals the destructive nature of his mind. That there is "no art / To find the mind's construction in the face" and that only time can show that construction is part of the tragedy of this play. Duncan, therefore, is the good king at one end of the play just as Malcolm is the good king at the other end of the play; the first has had his reign interrupted, and the second may have his reign interrupted, because in the nature of things some men succumb totally to the temptations of the devil.

Malcolm

Malcolm is the man who will be the ideal king, and thus he represents all that Macbeth as king is not. Malcolm uses deception only in a time of turmoil, when the values of fair and foul are confused. His deception, as he tells Macduff in IV.iii, is "modest wisdom" and therefore not to be used indiscriminately. When he feignedly denies his possession of the "king-becoming graces," he shows his understanding that these virtues in a king will bring his land "the sweet milk of concord." And when he finally confesses that he has been practicing a deception on Macduff and asserts an unspotted personal integrity, we realize that he does have the "king-becoming graces"; and that his behavior is meant to symbolize what a man in his position should do; and that when he becomes king he will rule with the "king-becoming graces" for the purpose of bringing his land "the sweet milk of concord." That he will in fact return Scotland to "wholesome days" is shown at the end both by his expressed intention and his usage of the imagery of time and growth.

Lady Macduff

Lady Macduff is a good woman who loves her husband and her family. When her husband flees Scotland without a word to her, she does not know what to think. Macduff seems to behave as the traitor he is accused of being. Yet, although she accuses him of not loving his family and of being a traitor, the prattling tone she uses with her son indicates that she does not quite believe what she says. Rather, her one scene indicates distress and confusion, not certainty of Macduff's motives. But all confusion is dispersed, of course, when the Murderers enter. She shows fierce loyalty to her husband and makes no attempt to save her own life at his expense. "Where is your husband?" demands one of the Murderers as he enters. "I hope in no place so unsanctified, / Where such as thou may'st find him," replies Lady Macduff without a thought for her life. In her distress and confusion, in her tenderness for her son, in her fierce loyalty to her husband Lady Macduff symbolizes the good and innocent people who are mindlessly slaughtered by the tyrant Macbeth.

ESSAY QUESTIONS AND MODEL ANSWERS

1. What is the theme of *Macbeth*?

Answer: By "the theme" of *Macbeth* one means the principal idea of the play, an idea that is seen in dramatic clothing probably in every act of the play. Abstracting a theme from a play is not identical to establishing a point as fact: an abstracter is working from the data of the play to an idea; therefore, he is working toward an opinion—others may form other opinions of a play's theme, and authors do not, as a rule, inform readers or audiences of their themes.

In *Macbeth*, as in other Shakespearean plays, we find that *appearances are one thing, reality is another*. This abstraction is too general to apply only to *Macbeth*. A more specific configuration of the main theme (there are also minor themes) of *Macbeth* is that *a man is deluded who thinks that he can play with evil and remain unchanged: mankind, yielding to evil, which of course appears to be good, is led to destruction.*

In Act I, this idea is embodied in Macbeth's and Lady Macbeth's response to the salutations of the Witches. Macbeth and his lady regard the greetings as Thane of Cawdor and future king as prophecies, and, further, with respect to the kingship, they contemplate murder of the incumbent, Duncan, although Macbeth is not told by the Witches to kill Duncan for his crown. In Act II, the Macbeths are deceived by the apparent ease and subsequent guiltlessness with which they can compass Duncan's death. They proceed in regicide, but Macbeth goes further than contemplated, because of his now-disturbed mind, to kill the two grooms. In Act III, Macbeth arranges the murder of Banquo and Fleance; but Fleance, who chiefly means the prospect of continuing Banquo's line, escapes. The murders of Banquo and Fleance had seemed to be assured, but the reality is otherwise. In Act IV and Act V, Macbeth wrongly reads the sayings of the Second and the Third Apparitions—the prophecies that "none of woman born / Shall harm Macbeth" and he is safe "until / Great Birnam Wood to high Dunsinane Hill / Shall come against him." Significantly he takes no particular notice of the saying of the First Apparition to "Beware Macduff." In Act V, these three oracular utterances come true as Macbeth learns to his horror when Malcolm's army, disguised by branches from Birnam Wood, comes against his castle and when Macduff, confronting Macbeth, informs him that he "was from his mother's womb / Untimely ripp'd" in Caesarian birth. Macbeth learns in death that appearances pointed one way, but reality, rock-hard, lay in the opposite direction. Against this rock he is crushed.

2. Explain the structure of *Macbeth*.

Response: The parts of a Shakespearean tragedy may be broken into the exposition, the development of conflict, the climax, the turning-point, the dénouement, and the catastrophe.

The exposition of *Macbeth* is relatively simple: we learn of battles involving Macbeth and Banquo against Macdonwald and his Hebrideans and against Sweno and his Norwegians. We also learn of the military distinction of these two Scottish captains and of the treachery of the Thane of Cawdor. With these intimations the exposition is virtually completed, and we rest for the moment to await developments.

Conflict in the dramatic sense swiftly begins with the Witches' greeting of Macbeth, having told him, "All hail, Macbeth, that shalt be King hereafter" and of Banquo with "Thou shalt get kings, though thou be none." Macbeth muses over the murder of his king, and his wife eggs him on. Inopportunely King

Duncan chooses to stay the night at Macbeth's castle. Duncan is dispatched, Macbeth is crowned, and in the banquet scene (III.iv), he convenes his nobles in a notable manner designed to elicit their good will toward him as king. But the Ghost of Banquo, whom Macbeth has caused to be murdered, religiously menaces him. Macbeth loses control of himself and alienates his wife in this, the scene of greatest tension in the play.

This is the *climax* and the *reversal* of Macbeth's fortunes. The *turning-point* is seen where, in viewing the tragedy as a whole, it is evident that one of the two forces is moving so that its triumph is assured, and so that no reconciliation is possible. In *Macbeth* the *turning-point* appears in III.vi where there is intelligence that a joint Scottish-English force will invade Scotland and cleanse the realm of Macbeth. The *dénouement* of *Macbeth*, a loosening of tension consequent upon the gradual fall of the protagonist from his apogee of control, is seen in Macbeth's need for further supernatural assurance (IV.i), the random killing of Lady Macduff and her offspring (IV.ii), the validation of Malcolm as King in the test with Macduff (IV.iii), the steeling of Macduff to a personal revenge on Macbeth (IV.iii), and the assault on Dunsinane by the Scottish-English forces. The *catastrophe* is of course the killing of Macbeth by Macduff.

3. How did *Macbeth* cater to King James I?

Answer: In several passages *Macbeth* is thought to caress King James I of England and VI of Scotland: Shakespeare could be unctuous toward reigning British royalty. The play presents Duncan as a divinely anointed king, "the Lord's anointed temple" (II.iii.73). In *Basilicon Doron: or His Maiesties Instructions to his Dearest Sonne, Henry the Prince*, James wrote that Henry should "learne to knowe and love that God, whometo ye have a double obligation; first, for that he made you a man; and next, for that he made you a little God to sitte on his throne, and rule other men." James was a published student of witchcraft (*Daemonologie* [1597]), and *Macbeth* is the first great

English play to take witches seriously. Scholars, *e.g.*, Henry N. Paul, *The Royal Play of Macbeth*, think James became skeptical of witches, approaching them, in his investigations, on the basis of whether any results came from their endeavors rather than from the question of whether witches were practicing or thought they were practicing the black art. But James never publicly repudiated his *Daemonologie*. *Macbeth*, to resume our answer, is a short play, perhaps half the length of *Hamlet*, because James would not sit through long plays. Furthermore, the Porter's allusion to the Gunpowder Plot of November 5, 1605 in the use of the word "equivocator" (among less obvious allusions)—a word thought applicable to Father Garnet, S. J., tried for complicity in this searing event on March 28, 1606—surely had the potency of awakening a drowsy James.

Macbeth notably caresses James on the point of ancestry. The King believed himself to be descended from both Banquo and Duncan, and he had been reminded of his descent from Banquo as well as of the imperial rule of his descendants in a playlet *Tres quasi Sibyllae* offered for his special delectation before St. John's College, Oxford, in 1605 during James's visit there. One should add that the Show of Kings in *Macbeth*, IV.i depicts James (to the cognoscenti) as the eighth king: James saw his simulacrum on the stage—something that should have started him—and this eighth king "bears a glass / Which shows me many more." Shakespeare tactfully removes Mary Queen of Scots, James's unhappy mother, from this show, Mary not being a king although she did rule in her own right.

In Lady Macbeth's sleepwalking scene (V.i), rehearsing the murder of Duncan, she exclaims, "Yet who would have thought the old man to have had so much blood in him?" This speech assigns preternaturally abundant blood to Duncan, an old man—old men in Shakespeare's plays conventionally have little blood. By this line it is suggested that Duncan in his old age possessed the power of begetting children who would resemble him (rather than their mother) because of his virtuous and blessed life, and James could infer that he was like his eminent ancestor. This listing does not exhaust matters that Shakespeare included in the play that he must have known to be interesting to his sovereign.

4. Describe Shakespeare's depiction of the Witches in *Macbeth*.

Response: The Witches of *Macbeth* were, we believe, taken seriously by the generality (although not the entirety) of Shakespeare's audience. Their credence was notably absent in the Restoration audience when "improvements" of *Macbeth* in the matter of Witches titillated these coterie playgoers. Even in today's world numerous persons proclaim themselves to be witches. Witches in Shakespeare's day were also called by other names, such as "nimphes," "feiries," "weirds." Unlike the fairies of *A Midsummer Night's Dream* they were associated with darkness and evil. The description "weird" in "weird sisters" came from Anglo-Saxon *wyrd*, "fate," although there is no evidence that Shakespeare knew this. He took the term "weird sisters" from his principal source for *Macbeth*, Holinshed's *Chronicles*, wherein they are called "goddesses of destinie." Shakespeare uses this conception of his Witches in I.ii, thereby lending them stature far above ordinary witches and assisting in deluding Macbeth to his downfall. When his destruction is at hand, Macbeth realizes that the Witches are "juggling fiends," creatures through whom the Devil works.

Interestingly, the great American Shakespearean scholar George Lyman Kittredge wrote: "The Weird Sisters, then, are the Norns of Scandinavian mythology. The Norns were goddesses who shaped beforehand the life of every man." If this view of *Macbeth* were credited, Macbeth would be deprived of free will, and so be different from Shakespeare's other tragic protagonists (except, perhaps, Romeo). In fact, *the Witches never indicate that they control Macbeth's destiny; at most they predict it.* No one in the play claims that they ordain human life.

On the other hand, if the Witches are regarded merely as figments of imagination (there is also the matter of Banquo's imagination), the play loses the idea that something in the universe is correspondent to something in the human soul: the Witches are not simply objectifications of Macbeth's evil desires and passions. Shakespeare keeps the Witches from being frivolous by exhibiting them in Macbeth only a few times; and their "masters," *i.e.*, devils, are not seen at all perhaps because the rather sublime devil and his angels had degenerated at the hands of dramatists into comic figures.

The Witches of *Macbeth* also differ from ordinary witches in that they can disappear into thin air. They seem to know the past, the present, and something of the future.

We do not know why the Hecate-scenes were introduced into *Macbeth*: one may guess that they were added to bring the play up to an average length or perhaps to make the play a little like a masque, a favorite Jacobean art form.

In his sorcery scenes Shakespeare uses trochaic tetrameter catalectic (—u / —u / —u /—) or headless octosyllabic couplets (— / u— / u— / u—), also used for fairy songs in *A Midsummer Night's Dream*. This meter gives a wild, doggerel effect.

The Witches employ this meter to elevate, render solemn, and induce obscure brevity in their communications to Macbeth, their inspiration being presumably of diabolic origin. Among themselves the Witches speak as if they came from the least educated classes.

Finally one may notice that Shakespeare does not associate the Black Mass with the Witches although some of their speech effects do mock the Holy Trinity. Once, however, they do adore their invisible devils—the closest Shakespeare ever came to staging idolatry in the grosser Old Testament sense.

FILM VERSIONS OF
MACBETH

According to Michael Mullin, "*Macbeth* on Film," *Film/Literature Quarterly*, 1 (1973), 332–342, there were at least nine different versions of *Macbeth* in the silent era, and there have been nine sound versions including adaptations. In his article, Mullin compares Orson Welles' *Macbeth*, Akira Kurosawa's *Throne of Blood*, George Schaefer's *Macbeth*, and Roman Polanski's *Macbeth*, four productions that are also discussed here.

Macbeth. *Directed by Orson Welles.* U. S. A. 1948 (rereleased 1949). Audio Brandon. Starring Orson Welles, Jeannette Nolan, Dan O'Herlihy.

This film is more Welles than Shakespeare. The setting is more that of *Beowulf* than that of the later Middle Ages or the Renaissance. On this account, Welles is impervious to elements in the play (the banquet, King Edward, hypocritical behavior) that suggest a highly developed culture against which the Macbeths do their dark deeds. Welles makes the conflict one between "agents of chaos, priests of hell and magic" and "Christian law and order." Christianity, we are told, has "newly arrived" on the Scottish moors. For the old order, Welles uses suggestions of Stonehenge and the Druids. Macbeth's appearance is as we might imagine Attila the Hun. All of this means, of course, that murder would be expected of Macbeth. Welles excises political elements intimating the union of Scotland and England and makes the play one of religious conflict: the major symbolism, accordingly, is the Celtic cross against the forked staffs of the Witches. Welles goes to the length of creating a character denominated the Holy Father, who is spiritually pitted against Witches that look like vulgar village gossips.

Basically, this film is an expressionist version of *Macbeth*: it rejects naturalism, reduces human relationships to "broad, primal urges," and expresses these by heavily symbolic gestures and postures. Thus, the shadow of Macbeth's finger moves slowly along a wall to point at Banquo's Ghost. The thrust of the film emanates from Welles' apprehension of a struggle in society between the individual will to power and the need for law and order.

Curiously, Lady Macbeth's dress has a zipper, and she uses lipstick.

Other discussion of this film may be found in James Naremore, "The Walking Shadow: Welles' Expressionist *Macbeth*," *Film/ Literature Quarterly*, 1 (1973), 360–366; Susan McCloskey, "Shakespeare, Orson Welles, and the 'Voodoo' *Macbeth*," *Shakespeare Quarterly*, 36 (1986), 406–416.

Throne of Blood. *Directed by Akira Kurosawa*. Japan. 1957. Audio Brandon. Starring Toshiro Mifune.

This film has been regarded as an adaptation rather than an imitation of Shakespeare. For example, without textual support Kurosawa makes the forest image central to the play: if Macbeth could control the forest he would be king indeed. Kurosawa's visual equivalents, such as having Macbeth die a pincushion of arrows, some of which have been shot by his own people, have been given qualified praise, *e.g.*, by John Gerlach, "Shakespeare, Kurosawa, and *Macbeth*: A Response to J. Blumenthal," *Film/ Literature Quarterly*, 1 (1973), 352–359. Kurosawa tries to make the corruption of Macbeth understandable by emphasizing the prophecies and the influence of his wife. Lady Macbeth announces her pregnancy, thus giving Macbeth a familial excuse for what in Shakespeare is less certainly realized. There are other instances of Kurosawa's chipping away something of the play's grasp of the darker aspects of human nature. Kurosawa's Macbeth, as the film goes on, becomes distanced from the viewers' sympathies and loses touch with the tragic idea of "a world that mocks human longing with sad knowledge of human limitations" (Gerlach).

Macbeth. *Directed by George Schaefer.* United Kingdom. 1960. Audio Brandon. Starring Maurice Evans and Judith Anderson.

This color version, critics say, suffers from "theatrical," "stagey" acting by Evans and Anderson and from the "prettifying" of costuming, the Witches, castles, and the heath, which become the bonny Scotland of the calendars. There is, to be sure, some slight textual support (in I.vi) where Duncan and Banquo remark on the "pleasant seat" of Macbeth's castle. The principal characters are too old for their parts, and too cheerful. There is undesirable contrast between the theatricality of the acting and the down-to-earthness or documentary quality of the scene and the innumerable bits of stage business. The emphasis on realism, as Michael Mullin has pointed out, causes the chubby Evans to appear as an "ageing psychopath" experiencing hallucinations instead of ghosts, visions, and incompletely glimpsed apparitions. The sympathy of the audience is withdrawn from Macbeth.

Macbeth. *Directed by Roman Polanski.* United Kingdom. 1971. Columbia Cinematheque. Starring Jon Finch and Francesca Annis.

Polanski's color version presents a young and attractive Macbeth and Lady Macbeth, who by these qualities help to realize the "fair is foul" theme of the play. Lady Macbeth is quite free from the meat-ax quality often associated with this character. Polanski—with memories of European concentration camps and the murder of his wife, Sharon Tate, by Manson and his "family"— emphasizes bloodshed more than Shakespeare does: for example, the camera focuses on the exceptionally bloody murder of Duncan whereas this act in Shakespeare's play takes place offstage. One gathers that for Polanski the crown itself is tainted because at the ending Donalbain, Malcolm's brother, is shown, *pace* Shakespeare, riding off to consult the Witches. Polanski sensationalizes Shakespeare's play by, among other things, having Macbeth drink the Witches' brew; by presenting the Witches nude in IV.i; by having Lady Macbeth appear nude in the sleepwalking scene; and by focusing the camera on the decapitation of Macbeth. The result is a rather melodramatic and distracting film.

Norman Berlin has reviewed the film in "*Macbeth*: Polanski and Shakespeare," *Film/Literature Quarterly*, 1 (1973), 291–298. David I. Grossvogel has written a review, "When the Stain Won't Wash: Polanski's *Macbeth*," *Diacritics: A Review of Contemporary Criticism*, 2 (Summer, 1972), 46–71.

AN ANNOTATED
BIBLIOGRAPHY ON
MACBETH

Allen, M. J. B. "Macbeth's Genial Porter." *English Literary Renaissance*, 4 (1974), 326–336.
Allen, after exploring the rich traditions of doors and porters, concludes that the Porter of II.iii is Macbeth's evil genius, and that the priapic lecher of the Porter's second speech is full of meaning for Macbeth. Allen is endeavoring to extend Harcourt's reading (see below).

Alspach, Russell K. "'Making the Green One Red,'" *Shakespeare Association Bulletin*, 16 (1941), 166–168.
Alspach argues for reading II.ii.60 "Making the green—one red" on the basis of the practice of Sheridan and Murphy and on the grounds that Renaissance men could see analogies between human blood and the sea.

Amneus, Daniel. "The Cawdor Episode in *Macbeth*," *Journal of English and Germanic Philology*, 63 (1964), 185–190.
Amneus views Macbeth's surprise at hearing of Cawdor's treachery as presenting no real difficulty, but he believes Ross's ignorance in I.iii impossible to reconcile with Ross's knowledge in I.ii as the text presently stands. He suggests a mental reconstruction that will restore order to a text whose obscurity is, he believes, of non-Shakespearean origin.

Amneus, Daniel. "Macbeth's 'Greater Honor,'" *Shakespeare Studies*, 6 (1970), 223–230.
Amneus studies the implications of I.iii.104 "a greater honor," concluding that Macbeth is to be named Prince of Cumberland.

He offers some points to support this supposition, such as Banquo's reaction, opinions of various scholars concerning textual dislocation and omission, the testimony of Simon Forman, and other matters.

Amneus, Daniel. "A Missing Scene in *Macbeth*," *Journal of English and Germanic Philology*, 60 (1961), 435–440.

Amneus argues on the basis of textual contradictions, chiefly significant in III.ii.8–12, that although the Folio places this passage before Banquo's murder, reason and Forman's report of *Macbeth* onstage in 1611 intimate that the passage should follow Banquo's murder. He concludes that it is highly probable that some cut material was reinserted in the play for non-Court performance.

Armstrong, W. A. "The Elizabethan Concept of the Tyrant," *Review of English Studies*, 22 (1946), 161–181.

This article studies Elizabethan theorizing on the nature of a tyrant. Armstrong concludes that Elizabethans drew a firm line between a usurper and a bad king who had lawfully succeeded to his throne and who was anointed. He cites the official *Homily against Disobedience, Cambises*, Charron, Bacon, Sidney, and others. Even though a legitimate king behaved like a tyrant, Elizabethans were counseled religiously to obey him. A tyrant had no such claim to obedience. Macbeth is a tyrant.

Arthos, John. "The Naive Imagination and the Destruction of Macbeth," *English Literary History*, 14 (1947), 114–126.

Arthos points out that the murder of Duncan marks a change in Macbeth's imagination: before that time, his images (which convey "truth" to him) were in the main personified; after that time the images are more and more frequently those of unpersonified matter. "Macbeth was either transformed into the likeness of the death his imagination materialized, or else he recognized them as the prophecy of what he was to become, matter bereft of life."

Babcock, Weston. "Macbeth's 'Cream-Fac'd Loone,'" *Shakespeare Quarterly*, 4 (1953), 199–202.

Babcock suggests that "cream-fac'd loon" in V.iii means the aquatic bird rather than "worthless fellow," the usual gloss. The

Oxford English Dictionary records this sense first in 1634. Babcock thinks it probable to have been current in oral English at the time of the composition of *Macbeth*. This suggestion makes a more vivid reading.

Bartholomeusz, Dennis. *Macbeth and the Players* (Cambridge: Cambridge Univ. Press, 1969).

Bartholomeusz' book is valuable to the student of *Macbeth* for its chronological review of broad conceptions and nuances in the acting of various roles in *Macbeth* including those of Burbage (so far as it can be gathered), Betterton, Garrick and Mrs. Pritchard, Sarah Siddons, Kemble, Macready, Irving, and others.

Berkeley, David Shelley. *Blood will Tell in Shakespeare's Plays* (Lubbock: Texas Tech University Press, 1984).

Berkeley explores the relationships between *blood* and *class* in Shakespeare's drama. He demonstrates Shakespeare's division of the human race into *gentles* and *base*, and remarks the characteristics, generally favorable for gentry and generally unfavorable for those without coats of arms. These conceptions bear on Lady Macbeth's (a gentlewoman's) *not* being stigmatized in the sleepwalking scene as giving blood to demons, as is Joan of Arc in I *Henry* VI. Shakespeare's very notable bias in favor of the gentles is seen also in young Macduff's close resemblance to his father, in the gold-red blood of Duncan, and in the preternatural amount of Duncan's blood, considering that he is an old man.

Biggins, Dennis. "'Appal' in *Macbeth*, III.iv.60," *English Language Notes*, 4 (1967), 259–261.

Biggins argues for the reading of *appal* in III.iv.60 as "to make pale" rather than "to dismay."

Biggins, Dennis. "Scorpions, Serpents, and Treachery in *Macbeth*," *Shakespeare Studies*, 1 (1965), 29–36.

Biggins presents a medieval and Renaissance background for the idea, relative to III.ii.36, that scorpions were emblematic of deceitful and flattering treachery. Scorpions were thought to be serpents, and the Devil was the archetypal scorpion-serpent. Biggins finds much irony in Macbeth's playing both snake and scorpion to Duncan and then finding a serpent under every innocent flower. Two additional pieces of scholarship to be examined in this connection are Clifford Davidson, "Full of Scorpions is My Mind," *Times Literary Supplement*, Nov. 4, 1965, p. 988, in which the scorpion is held to be a Judas symbol, and Dennis Biggins, "Full of Scorpions," *Times Literary Supplement*, Feb. 10, 1966, p. 110.

Biggins, Dennis. "Sexuality, Witchcraft and Violence in *Macbeth*." *Shakespeare Studies*, 8 (1975), 255–277.

Biggins canvasses the numerous sexual references and allusions in *Macbeth*. The focus of his study is to understand the depiction of the Witches in one of the traditional trappings of their kind and, more importantly, to indicate Macbeth's and Lady Macbeth's violent tendencies in terms of aberrant and unfruitful sexual behavior.

Blissett, William, "The Secret'st Man of Blood. A Study of Dramatic Irony in *Macbeth*," *Shakespeare Quarterly*, 10 (1959), 397–408.

Blissett's article is suggestive of the survival of certain prescientific ideas of long history that illuminate portions of *Macbeth*. For example, Duncan's "drops of sorrow" intimate not weakness but the ability in old age to reproduce. Banquo's hair is a sign, semen being thought by some to be stored in the head, of the abundance of blood in him that suggests his "genius," his "genial power" to beget a prolific family. Blissett sees the Macbeths as staining their minds by willingly inhaling the "ensanguined mist" in which they are enveloped. More historical and literary documentation would have improved the article.

Blythe, Joan H. "'His Horses Go About': The Circumstance of Banquo's Death and the Escape of Fleance." *Notes and Queries*, 21 (1974), 131–132.

Blythe offers reasons why murderers on foot are able to kill an armed thane, whom some might assume to be mounted, and therefore with his mounted son be able to resist his death.

Bradbrook, Muriel C., "The Sources of *Macbeth*," *Shakespeare Survey 4* (Cambridge: Cambridge Univ. Press, 1951), 35–38.

In this article Bradbrook traces the sources of several ingredients of *Macbeth* with particular attention to their political implications, usually meaning their relationship to King James. For example, Malcolm's practice of dissimulation with Macduff is related to James's being obliged to practice dissimulation as a youth of eighteen following the Ruthven Raid of 1582.

Bradley, A. C. *Shakespearean Tragedy. Lectures on Hamlet, Othello, King Lear, Macbeth.* 2nd ed., reprinted (New York: St. Martins, 1965).

Bradley's seminal work, often reprinted and much used for student cribbing, undertakes, among other things, to define the nature of Shakespearean tragedy. Discussing *Macbeth* as one of Shakespeare's four great tragedies, Bradley focuses attention on our experience of *Macbeth* as art rather than upon the play on the boards or on the page; in other words, he is primarily interested in subjective reactions. Bradley sees Macbeth, like other Shakespearean protagonists, as possessing "a marked one-sidedness," which is his flaw. The impression of Macbeth's career is one of waste, a conception associated with the nineteenth-century secularist idea of Creative Evolution, which is not clearly part of Shakespeare's world. Bradley emphasizes the point that Macbeth never entirely loses our sympathy: "In the very depths a gleam of his native love of goodness, and with it a touch of tragic grandeur rests upon him." Bradley considers Macbeth as being independent of his world. He regards Banquo as compromising himself. Bradley has been so successful in his study of character that, as Muir says, "Bradley's conception of the characters is still an orthodoxy to be questioned." Bradley is better at defining *Macbeth's* structure: exposition, crisis or turning-point, "fourth-act problem," catastrophe, etc. He faults *Macbeth* for being choppy in Act V with its stringing together of short scenes. This author is excellent on the peculiar atmosphere of the play—one of a horrid "darkness, the lights and colors that illuminate it, the storm that rushes through it, the violent and gigantic images," the repellent ingredients of the cauldron, the cannibal horses, and much else.

Brindley, D. J. "Reversal of Values in *Macbeth*," *English Studies in Africa*, 6–8 (1963), 137–143.

Brindley studies reversals of values in *Macbeth* under four headings—natural, sexual, moral, and spiritual. The play at last corrects these disorders.

Brooks, Cleanth. "The Naked Babe and the Cloak of Manliness," *The Well Wrought Urn: Studies in the Structure of Poetry* (New York: Reynal S. Hitchcock [1947]).

Brooks analyzes the babe image in Lady Macbeth's speech in I.vii.54–59, in Macbeth's image of "pity like a naked, newborn babe . . . ," in the apparition of the Weird Sisters, and in the murder of Macduff's children. He regards the babe as a symbol of the future, of purposes that give meaning to life, and of ties that make man human. Lady Macbeth in her overweening desire to control the future is willing, if need be, to kill her own child; and she tries to wean Macbeth of his unmanly pity, *i.e.*, the compassion of which the babe is a symbol.

Brown, Beatrice. "Exemplum Materials Underlying *Macbeth*," *Publications of the Modern Language Association*, 50 (1935), 700–714.

The author deals with stories of bloodstained hands, omens at ceremonial feasts, and so forth, which although not regarded as directly influencing Shakespeare, yet "underlie" certain incidents in *Macbeth*.

Bryant, J. A., Jr. *Hippolyta's View: Some Christian Aspects of Shakespeare's Plays* (Lexington: Univ. of Kentucky Press, 1961).

J. A. Bryant, Jr. in the chapter of *Macbeth* connects certain Bible verses with the thought and action of *Macbeth*. Perhaps his most cogent conflations are the analogy between the fantastic storm that accompanies the death of Duncan and the storm reported in Matt. 27, 51–52 following the death of Jesus; and Macbeth's sleeplessness in the light of Proverbs 3, 24, "When thou liest down, thou shalt not be afraid; yea, thou shalt lie down, and thy sleep shall be sweet."

Coffin, Tristram. "Folk Logic and the Bard: Act I of *Macbeth*" in *Medieval Literature and Folklore Studies: Essays in Honor of Francis Lee Utley*, ed. Jerome Mandel and Bruce A. Rosenberg (New Brunswick, N. J.: Rutgers Univ. Press, 1970), pp. 331–343.

Coffin, treating iii.130–141; iv.48–53; v.1–30; v.39 ff.; v.60–71; and vi.1 ff., makes the point that *Macbeth* is a primitive folk story; as such, it is not concerned with tying up loose ends, something that Coffin suggests is an unnecessary application of logical and technological thought to the ancient art of story-telling.

Cormican, L. A. "Medieval Idiom in Shakespeare," *Scrutiny*, 17 (1950–51), 186–202, 298–317.
This important article states: "Shakespeare's gradual transition from the

> Taffeta phrases, silken terms precise,
> Three-pil'd hyperboles, spruce affectation,
> Figures pedantical

to the 'blanket of the night,' and the 'rank sweat of an unseamed bed' is much more than a growth in literary power or an expansion of dramatic talent; it is the full employment, for the first and last time, of the medieval ethos and medieval ethic in order to enrich and diversify the material of tragedy." *Macbeth*, Cormican says, makes fullest use of interaction between the physical and the metaphysical worlds. This scholar commends Shakespeare for his tact in hitting an effective mean between blatant obviousness in dealing with the supernatural and simply denying forces of the other world. He attributes the brevity of *Macbeth* to Shakespeare's drawing upon beliefs and feelings of the Medieval–Renaissance mentality, such as those nourished by the Psalms and the Book of Common Prayer. Generally, Cormican points to belief in the sacredness of material objects, especially the human body, the blending of the personal and common values, the reality of Hell, the working of Providence through human free will, the existence of angels and demons, the eternal implications of impenitence, all of which are relevant to *Macbeth*.

Coursen, Herbert R., Jr. "In Deepest Consequence: *Macbeth*." *Shakespeare Quarterly*, 18 (1967), 375–388.
This paper is an attempt to connect the power and intensity of *Macbeth* with its exploitation of one of the original "myths"— a fall from grace, which is still relevant and still full of truth.

Coursen canvasses the flower and the serpent (I.v.66–67), allusions to fallen angels, Lilith and Eve within Lady Macbeth, Dunsinane as Eden (I.vi.1–10). These forces (and others) well up through the play and oblige us to see "a gigantic reflexion of our sinful selves thrown upon the immeasurable screen of the universe" (Dover Wilson).

Coursen, Herbert R., Jr. "Malcolm and Edgar," *Discourse*, 2 (1968), 430–438.

Coursen closely examines Malcolm's manipulation of Macduff, contrasting it with Edgar's manipulation of Gloucester in *King Lear*. He finds this matter reveals Malcolm's fitness to be king and that, although appearances are to the contrary, "a purposive cosmos" overrules Scotland.

Cunningham, Dolora G. "*Macbeth*: The Tragedy of the Hardened Heart," *Shakespeare Quarterly*, 14 (1963), 39–47.

By pointing to evidences of Macbeth's remnants of human and divine nature even well along in his career of bloodshed, Cunningham supplies a corrective to that oversimplified view of the protagonist which characterizes him as finally being no more than a bloody butcher. She points out two alternatives to Macbeth's final way of life—death or heavenly forgiveness suggested by Macduff in IV.iii.

Cutts, John P. "Till Birnam Forest Come to Dunsinane," *Shakespeare Quarterly*, 21 (1970), 497–499.

Cutts points out that George Sandys in his commentary to *Ovid's Metamorphosis Englished, Mythologized, and Represented in Figures* . . . (1632) regarded the moving of Birnam Wood as a latter-day example of Orpheus' music in calming the Bacchides. Cutts suggests that the order and ceremony of his proceeding supports Malcolm's restoration to his father's throne in kingly dignity rather than in mad vengeance.

Daly, Peter M. "Of *Macbeth*, Martlets and Other 'Fowles of Heaven,'" *Mosaic*, 12 (1978), 23–46.

Daly observes, "Shakespeare and his contemporaries still lived in a world in which an object of nature could be regarded as embodying meaning, stamped into its qualities, form, and actions by the Creator." This learned essay on folkloristic and scholarly associations of martins (and other birds in *Macbeth*) presents many meanings, some not notably relevant, that Banquo's "martlets" in *Macbeth*, I.vi might have. The article is independently good for understanding the Renaissance emblem.

Darroll, G. M. H. "The Tragic Stupidity," *English Studies in Africa*, 5 (1962), 49–58.

Darroll sensitively studies Lady Macbeth. He dismisses A. C. Bradley's conception of her as a hatchet-like, unfeminine creature who goads her husband into crime, and suggests, probably mistakenly, that this understanding of the role may derive from the acting of Mrs. Siddons. Darroll points to the close relationship of Macbeth and Lady Macbeth at the beginning of the play: he observes that Macbeth uses "dear" or "dearest" in addressing his wife, something unusual among Shakespeare's husbands. Lady Macbeth's tragic flaw is seen as loyalty to her husband that is so blind and so fierce that it amounts to self-murder. Interestingly, he points out that the Porter's word "equivocator" may be applied to Lady Macbeth's euphemisms like "this great deed" which mean the murder of Duncan.

Davidson, Clifford. "The Witches' Dances in *Macbeth*," *Shakespeare Newsletter*, 18 (1968), 37.

Davidson gives references for the idea that the Witches' dances in Act IV of *Macbeth* were adapted for popular performances from an antimasque in Jonson's *Masque of Queenes* (1609). He also gives references for music used in these dances.

Draper, John W. "The 'Gracious Duncan,'" *Modern Language Review*, 36 (1941), 495–499.

Draper argues for the theory that Duncan is a sanguine man as understood in Galenic medicine. Duncan's mistakes in lacking caution and in declining evasive action are due to too much blood in his system.

Dyson, J. P. "The Structural Function of the Banquet Scene in *Macbeth*," *Shakespeare Quarterly*, 14 (1963), 369–378.

Dyson regards the banquet scene as presenting in little the movement in Macbeth's mind and in his society from order to chaos.

Elliott, G. R. *Dramatic Providence in Macbeth* (Princeton: Princeton Univ. Press, 1958).

Like Elliott's books on *Hamlet* (*Scourge and Minister*, 1951) and *Othello* (*Flaming Minister*, 1953), this work presents the author's interpretations scene by scene, speech by speech. The book is worth reading despite the fact that few Renaissance authors are marshalled, and despite some interpretations, *e.g.*, that Macbeth is subdued into "actual penitence" by Macduff.

Fergusson, Sir James. *The Man Behind Macbeth* (London: Faber and Faber, 1969).

Sir James argues that since *Macbeth* deals with the Scotland of the sixteenth rather than the eleventh century, Shakespeare may have colored the characterization of Macbeth with stories of James Stewart, second son to Lord Ochiltree, and the characterization of Lady Macbeth with the notoriety of Stewart's wife, Elizabeth. Calling attention to the similarities of Stewart's eloquence, his tyranny, and his violent temper, Fergusson states: "Macbeth becomes Thane of Glamis, Thane of Cawdor, and finally King. Stewart became Earl of Arran, acquired the lands that had been Gowrie's and aspired to be 'King James the Seventh'. Macbeth killed Banquo and tried to kill Macduff and 'seize upon Fife' from fear of their rebelling against him. Stewart compassed the death of Drumquhassill and Mains for the same reason. Macbeth was slain by Macduff, Stewart by Torthorwald, both in revenge. Stewart like Macbeth was deceived by 'juggling fiends', and his severed head was displayed on a lance as was Macbeth's (in Holinshed) on a pole." If Shakespeare used Stewart to color Macbeth, it would be only natural to use Lady Arran to flesh out the mere suggestion of her character in Holinshed. Lady Arran trafficked in witchcraft, and a point of connection to Lady Macbeth is the latter's invocation to the powers of evil. Both left storied reputations as evildoers. Fergusson speculates that Shakespeare heard of James Stewart through the actor Laurence Fletcher.

Fiske, Roger. "The 'Macbeth' Music," *Music & Letters*, 45 (1964), 114–125.

This article discusses scores and composers for music used in

the eighteenth and nineteenth centuries to enrich productions of
Macbeth.

Fox, Alice. "Obstetrics and Gynecology in *Macbeth*,"
Shakespeare Studies. 12 (1979), 127–141.
This article dwells upon the many suggestions of childbirth both
normal and abortive, of pregnancy, and other gynecological
matters in *Macbeth* read with attention to the thought of
Shakespeare's times on these subjects. Fox believes that the
Macbeths are repeatedly frustrated in their attempts to have
children, the preoccupation of the play's imagery of obstetrics
and gynecology pointing this way.

Free, William J. "Shakespeare's MACBETH, III, iv, 122–126
and IV, i, 90–84," *Explicator*, 19 (1961), item 50.
Free points out the irony of juxtaposing III.iv.122–126 and
IV.i.90–94. In the earlier passage Macbeth as a man of conscience thinks that stones would move and trees would speak
out against murder. In the latter Macbeth expresses disbelief,
with regard to the prophecy concerning Birnam Wood, that
trees could move. The collocation suggests that his "spiritual
tragedy is complete."

Frye, Roland M. "'Out, Out, Brief Candle,' and the Jacobean
Understanding," *Notes and Queries*, N. S. 2 (1955), 143–145.
Frye collects Elizabethan and Jacobean analogues to Macbeth's
"brief candle" speech. Authors cited are Donne, Anthony
Copley, John Bradford, Archbishop Grindal, Richard Brath-
wait. Frye says, "Donne's description of that human light which
'does not so much as portend or signify anything; furnish[es] the
final gloss on Macbeth's view of life as 'signifying nothing.'"

Frye, Roland M. "Theological and Non-Theological Structures
in Tragedy," *Shakespeare Studies*. 4 (1968), 132–148.
Comparing Marlowe's *Doctor Faustus* and *Macbeth*, Frye
holds that the Marlovian play is inherently theological whereas
Macbeth is primarily ethical. He points out that the comparison
is justified because Shakespeare made more significant use of
theological material in *Macbeth* than in his other tragedies. One
point of contrast is the prominence of theological discussion in

Faustus and the minimal use of such reference in *Macbeth*. Faustus's mind is frequently focused on Christ, but in *Macbeth* the Name is not mentioned. Faustus wants to be more than man; Macbeth wants to found a Scottish dynasty. Faustus recommits the original sin; Macbeth sins in the sense that every sin is the issue of original sin.

Gent, Lucy. "The Self-Cozening Eye," *Review of English Studies*, 34 (1983), 419–428.

This article speculatively explores visual equivocation in *Macbeth*, making much of Macbeth's victimization as expressed in his aside "Nothing is but what is not" (I.iii.141). ". . . 'what is not' is a classic Augustinian definition of evil; in Macbeth's world by this point reality is becoming shaped by evil, defined as 'what is not', replacing what actually has existence, a moral world shaped by a benign creator."

Goode, Bill. "How Little the Lady Knew Her Lord: A Note on *Macbeth*," *American Imago*, 20 (1963), 349–356.

Goode regards Lady Macbeth as a wife who is exploited by her husband, particularly seen in the evidences of her having a moral conscience and of his possessing only a prudential counterpart of one. Macbeth goes to lengths in bloodletting that she has never contemplated. She absorbs full guilt for all the murders committed by her husband, and she breaks under the strain.

Harcourt, John B., "'I Pray You, Remember the Porter,'" *Shakespeare Quarterly*, 12 (1961), 393–402.

Harcourt points out that the Porter scene in *Macbeth* (II.iii) has undergone a vast change in interpretation from Pope, Hanmer, and Coleridge, who thought all of it or most of it unworthy of Shakespeare, to present-day criticism, which finds it authentically Shakespearian and thematically significant. Harcourt finds the farmer, the equivocator, and the tailor to have affinities with Macbeth: ". . . if we consider that Macbeth, driven by a ruthless personal ambition, has committed the ultimate in treason, regicide, and has seized the crown and royal robes that were not his by right, it becomes evident that the Porter's three examples were chosen not at random, but precisely because of their relevance to the dramatic situation." The scene deglamorizes Macbeth, and it suggests his unhappy ending. It plays upon the differences between appearances and reality, and it suggests that time sides with the forces of justice. The Porter's dealing with fornication and drunkenness—sins having some degree of human warmth—and his commenting on the coldness of the Scottish castle underscore Macbeth's monstrosity in evil. Harcourt continues with suggestions of the Harrowing of Hell in the scene with the Porter as a devil-figure and Macduff as a Christ-figure.

Harding, D. W. "Women's Fantasy of Manhood: A Shakespearian Theme," *Shakespeare Quarterly*, 20 (1969), 245–253.
This article views Macbeth as abjuring his own prudential understanding that even a bloody, bold, and resolute man lives in a world where some other men are also bloody, bold, and resolute, and as surrendering to his wife's fantasy that all her husband needs to succeed is unscrupulous aggressiveness. Harding points up Lady Macbeth's essential femininity and consequent inability to enter into the masculine thought-world.

Hawkins, Michael. "History, Politics, and *Macbeth*," *Focus on Macbeth*, ed. John R. Brown (London: Routledge & Kegan Paul, 1982), pp. 155–182.
Hawkins points out that Macbeth responds to four emphases of fifteenth- and sixteenth-century political discussion: he is active; he is a free agent; he knows the future because the Witches do not tell him lies (their statements are given "a compatible, if alternative, meaning"); he "is successful while he works with the prophecies, unsuccessful when he tries to thwart them."

Heilman, Robert B. "The Criminal as Tragic Hero: Dramatic Methods," *Shakespeare Survey 19* (Cambridge: Cambridge Univ. Press, 1966), pp. 12–24.
Heilman suggests that in the first two acts of *Macbeth*, Shakespeare causes the reader perhaps to collude with a criminal, to give way to envy and ruthless ambition, to experience pleasure in securing the fruits of *virtù*; certainly the reader is led to experience exposure, anxiety, detection, insomnia and night-

mares, the need for safety, the feeling of having made a bad bargain, the pain of struggling against odds, and the rapid coming of old age. In the last acts Macbeth's personality "contracts"—he "seems to discard large areas of consciousness as he goes, to shrink from multilateral to unilateral being." Since Macbeth does not reckon with himself morally, the play does not in this respect reach the heights of Shakespeare's other tragedies.

Henderson, Archibald, "Macbeth as Underdog: Central Villain, Tragic Hero," *Forum*, 4 (1967), 14–17.

This paper argues that audience sympathy is with Macbeth because he is an "underdog." The author magnifies Duncan's gaucheries and bad timing, but he goes beyond reason in suggesting that Duncan wishes to take possession of Macbeth's castle and Lady Macbeth. This article seems to be dominated by the Romantic notion that sympathy goes to the protagonist simply because he is the underdog and without regard to considerations of merit.

Holloway, John. *The Story of the Night* (Lincoln: Univ. of Nebraska Press, 1961), pp. 57–74.

Holloway approaches *Macbeth* as myth or ritual with basic analogies to the Christian view of the play. He regards Macbeth as "a scapegoat, a lord of misrule who has turned life into riot for his limited time, and is then driven out and destroyed by the forces which embody the fertile vitality and the communal happiness of the social group." Holloway emphasizes the emblematical images of the bloody man, the armed rider, the violent horses as spreading disruption, violence, and monstrosity over the communal life of man.

Hunter, William B., Jr. "A Decorous *Macbeth*." *English Language Notes*, 8 (1971), 169–173.

Hunter canvasses the text of *Macbeth* with regard to the deaths of Banquo, the Macduffs, Seyward, and Macbeth, concluding that the directions are so ambiguous that the deaths may occur on the stage or off. Offstage murder is classically decorous; onstage killing is what ordinary theatre-goers wanted.

Huntley, Frank L. "*Macbeth* and the Background of Jesuitical

Equivocation," *Publications of the Modern Language Association*, 79 (1964), 390–400.

Huntley traces the background of the doctrine of equivocation to Sir Edward Coke's definition in 1606 and, more importantly, to the *Treatise of Equivocation*. This article is valuable for its careful elucidation of the doctrine and for the application of the doctrine of the Porter's scene. A. E. Malloch in "Some Notes on Equivocation," *PMLA*, 81 (1966), 145–146, offers several corrections to the historical parts of Huntley's article, tracing the origin of the doctrine to Martin Azpilcueta, the authorship of the *Treatise of Equivocation* to Garnet, and the appropriation (rather than the development of the doctrine) by the Jesuits.

Jorgensen, Paul A. *Our Naked Frailties: Sensational Art and Meaning in Macbeth* (Berkeley: Univ. of California Press, 1971).

Jorgensen studies the nature of the "sensational" in *Macbeth* in the primary sense of causing sensation and to a lesser extent in the popular meaning of the spectacular. Much of what he deals with is well known in scholarship or obvious in the play, but occasional observations are notable for personal insight. For example, he states that Macbeth and Lady Macbeth speak of evil with heavy reliance upon "it" and other pronouns without antecedents. There are valuable remarks upon Shakespeare's distancing us from violence, something ignored by Polanski in his filmed version. Jorgensen traces the ritualistic qualities of Duncan's murder to the practice of Seneca. He assesses the comparative innocence of Macbeth and Lady Macbeth at the time of the murder of Duncan.

Jaarsma, Richard J. "The Tragedy of Banquo," *Literature and Psychology*, 17 (1967), 87–94.

Jaarsma writes in support of Bradley's view that Banquo's character changes for the worse: Banquo becomes, he says, Macbeth's silent accomplice. The author makes much of Banquo's "cursed thoughts that nature / Gives way to in repose!" (II.i.6–9).

Jack, Jane H. "Macbeth, King James, and The Bible," *English Literary History*, 22 (1955), 173–193.

Jack, viewing *Macbeth* as a probing of evil described in Biblical terms, sees the narrative of Macbeth largely in terms of Old Testament stories concerning the allegiance of certain kings to false prophets rather than to the true God. Accordingly she makes explicit parallels between Saul and Macbeth. Her emphasis implies a subordination of ideas in the play on order and degree and on Scottish and English history. In this article much is made concerning the community of ideas derived from the Bible in King James's *Daemonologie*, *Basilikon Doron*, and *Sermon on Revelation* and themes and images of tyranny, light and darkness, withdrawal of divine grace, witchcraft, and blood in *Macbeth*.

Jaech, Sharon L. J. "Political Prophecy and Macbeth's 'Sweet Bodements,'" *Shakespeare Quarterly*, 34 (1983), 290–297.
Jaech observes early English use of political prophecies attributed to Merlin, Thomas à Becket, Thomas of Erceldoune, and others. Shakespeare has such a prophecy in *King Lear*. She concludes that "the armed head, the bloody child, and the crowned child would have been recognized as vivid images of death, destruction, and ultimate deliverance."

Kantak, V. Y. "An Approach to Shakespearian Tragedy: The 'Actor' Image in *Macbeth*," *Shakespeare Survey 16* (Cambridge: Cambridge Univ. Press, 1963), pp. 42–52.
This article is valuable for mediating between A. C. Bradley's emphasis upon Shakespeare's characters as being living persons and the New Critics' tendency to regard them as vehicles of symbolic force, seeing *Macbeth*, for example, as a medieval morality play with characters as symbols for Christian virtues and vices. Kantak observes Banquo's speech of "the temple-haunting martlet" as, with Bradley, reflecting the speaker's characterization at the time and as, with the New Critics, contributing enrichment to the play's thematic content.

Kirsch, Arthur. "Macbeth's Suicide," *English Literary History*, 51 (1984), 269–296.
Kirsch develops the self-centeredness of Macbeth, invoking Montaigne and Freud as lending insight into this subject. The most valuable part of this paper is the connection between

Macbeth and *The Rape of Lucrece*, "perhaps its [*Macbeth*'s] most deeply suggestive source."

Kirschbaum, Leo. "Banquo and Edgar: Character and Function," *Essays in Criticism*, 7 (1957), 2–8.

Kirschbaum wrote this article, as against Bradley's view of Banquo as a whole man, as a psychologically valid being, to demonstrate that Banquo is at all points a foil to Macbeth. Perhaps his most telling point is made in correction of Bradley's view of III.i.1–10 in which the elder critic thought Banquo to have yielded to evil: "Hush! no more," observes Kirschbaum, is not said to dismiss "cursed thoughts," but merely to register Banquo's hearing of trumpets heralding the entrance of the King and Queen. Kirschbaum argues for the symbolic quality of Banquo's characterization.

Knight, G. Wilson. *The Imperial Theme* (London: Methuen, 1951).

Knight studies the opposition of themes in *Macbeth*. The life-themes are 1. Warrior-honor, 2. Imperial magnificence, 3. Sleep and Feasting, 4. Ideas of creation and nature's innocence. Themes of evil are 1. Death and ill omen, 2. Darkness, 3. Disorder.

Knight, G. Wilson. "*Macbeth* and the Metaphysic of Evil," *The Wheel of Fire*, rev. ed. (London: Methuen, 1949), pp. 140–159.

Knight considers *Macbeth* as a tragedy presenting disorder and confusion—Macbeth's "ambition" is only a name for something less consciously realized. He calls attention to questionings, rumors, fears, horrible imaginings, unreality, disorder in the form of ugly and ominous animals, smeary blood. He takes the unusual view that at the end, Macbeth "has won through by excessive crime to an harmonious and honest relation with his surroundings." The assertion of good through Malcolm "brings him peace."

Knights, L. C. *Some Shakespearean Themes* (London: Chatto and Windus, 1959).

Knights' article makes much of the two kinds of nature in *Macbeth*—that kind in humanity and external nature that is associated with creativity and concord, and the other kind associated with violence, monstrosity, and abnormality. If man acknowledges his own humanity, he aligns himself with nature in the good sense. *Macbeth* is therefore a document opposed to that element of Jacobean pessimism asserting the naturalness of evil.

Kocher, Paul H. "Lady Macbeth and the Doctor," *Shakespeare Quarterly*, 5 (1954), 341–349.
Kocher undertakes to show that Lady Macbeth suffers not from demon-possession but from purely material maladies.

Lyle, E. B. "Two Parallels in *Macbeth* to Seneca's *Hercules Oetaeus*," *English Studies*, 53 (1972), 109–112.
The passages for which Senecan parallels are offered, for which borrowing is modestly suggested, are III.iv.99–105 and III.i.63–67.

Mates, Julian. "Macbeth's Head," *American Notes and Queries*, 10 (1971), 152–153.
Mates points out that Jacobeans would regard the poled head of Macbeth as a symbol of treachery because "All Londoners were familiar with heads atop the southern gate towers of London Bridge, the heads of those executed as traitors."

McCarthy, Mary. "General Macbeth," *Harper's Magazine* 224 (June, 1962), 35–39.
Ms. McCarthy takes the view that Macbeth is analogous to a bourgeois type: he trusts himself rather than fate, he is not clever, he is envious, he lacks feeling for others, his "scruples" are prudential, his soliloquies are only rhetoric. He does not make himself an utter monster because he declines to "unsex" himself.

McGee, Arthur, "'Macbeth' and the Furies," *Shakespeare Survey 19* (Cambridge: Cambridge Univ. Press, 1966), pp. 55–67.
McGee holds that the Elizabethan understanding or "image" of witches compounded the Furies of classical literature, Biblical demons, and the fairies of folklore. This "plasticity" permitted use of materials so widely diverse to our minds as materials from the North Berwick witch trials (in I.iii) and Hecate. The Weird Sisters, he thinks, tempt Macbeth and strive to produce

remorse and despair. They cause the thunder, lightning, fog, the airborne dagger, Banquo's Ghost, the eclipse of the sun, the drawing down of the moon, nightmares; and they are associated with owl-symbolism and an atmosphere suggesting the end of the world. McGee thinks that Macbeth's ambition and despair should be traced to Satan, the Day of Judgment, and Hell as objective realities instead of being restricted to the subjective processes of characterization.

Merchant, W. Moelwyn, "'His Fiend-Like Queen,'" *Shakespeare Survey 19* (Cambridge: Cambridge Univ. Press, 1966), pp. 75–81.

Merchant points out that Lady Macbeth's voluntary invitation to demons to possess her (he is particularly convincing on the meaning of "take" in "take my milk for all") dramatically contrasts with the slow operations of mind, conscience, and imagination that bring Macbeth to evil.

Morris, Brian. "The kingdom, the power, and the glory in *Macbeth*," *Focus on Macbeth*, ed. John R. Brown (London: Routledge & Kegan Paul, 1982), pp. 30–33.

Morris observes that there is nothing of repentance and suing for Grace in *Macbeth*: Macbeth "never envisages that by Sin he has grieved God's heart of love." The play possesses the unique tone of alternating between courtesy, which Morris regards as "the highest moral value in the play, or at least its most central and respected value," and violence.

Murdoch, Dugald, "The Thane of Cawdor and Macbeth," *Studia Neophilologica*, 43 (1971), 221–226.

Murdoch sensibly discusses the problem of the Thane of Cawdor, specifically stated by Dr. Johnson concerning I.iii: "Neither Ross knew what he had just reported, nor Macbeth knew what he had just done." Murdoch points out the assumptions and presuppositions upon which this judgment rests, concluding that it is unwarranted. He is disposed to view the matter as deliberate creation of an atmosphere of doubt, uncertainty, and vagueness: hence it is justifiable on dramatic grounds.

Murray, W. A., "Why Was Duncan's Blood Golden?" *Shakespeare Survey 19* (Cambridge: Cambridge Univ. Press, 1966), pp. 34–44.

Murray explains Duncan's "golden blood" as a vision based on the concept of alchemical tincture, "an enormously strong colouring agent made of perfected matter, which has the power of transmuting substances. . . ." Duncan's blood is golden because "it is already in the hand of God"; "it is part of the perfection of heaven."

Murry, John Middleton. *Shakespeare* (London: Cape, 1936, rtd. 1948).

In the chapter "The Time Has Been" Murry states that for Macbeth and Lady Macbeth to "see themselves, with an absolute and terrible naiveté . . . convinces us . . . of their essential nobility of soul." Murry believes that Shakespeare leaves unanswered the question of whether the Witches have power over Macbeth. He concentrates on the naive but terrible remarks Macbeth and his lady make upon the spur of the developing action.

Nielsen, Elizabeth, "Post Shakespearian Actor," *Shakespeare Quarterly*, 16 (1965), 193–199.

This article is valuable for bidding us to keep the law of tanistry in mind in interpreting *Macbeth*: the law that made the Scottish succession not directly hereditary but elective within the branches of the "blood royal." Duncan ignores this law in designating Malcolm as "Prince of Cumberland." In short, Macbeth has before him the memory of Scottish kings killing and being killed. He has rights to the throne, and his wife also is the blood royal. Thus, the situation enlists his mind in the direction of evil and his conscience in the direction of declining to join the murderous procession of preceding Scottish kings and claimants to the throne.

Nosworthy, J. S. "The Hecate Scenes in *Macbeth*," *Review of English Studies*, 24 (1948), 138–139.

Nosworthy points up differences between Middleton's and Shakespeare's treatments of Hecate. He suggests that Hecate's first speech is an allusion "not to the early scenes but to previous performances of the play which were the poorer (or the richer) for her absence." Hecate seems to have been much appreciated in the seventeenth century.

Orrell, John. "The Bellman in *Macbeth*, II.ii.3," *Notes and Queries*, N. S. 13 (1966), 138.

Orrell points out that in *Blurt, Master Constable* (1602) one finds the following lines: ". . . the Owle, whose voice / Shreikes, like the Bell-man in the Loueres ears."

Parker, Barbara L. "*Macbeth*: The Great Illusion," *Sewanee Review*, 78 (1970), 476–487.

In this study of the dichotomy between the real and the illusory in *Macbeth*, perhaps the most valuable point is the contrast between time in terms of planting and harvesting—the real—as seen in some of the speeches of Duncan and Banquo, and time in terms of prophecy—the illusory—seen in speeches of the Witches and Lady Macbeth (I.v.56–58). The play's ending sees the restoration of natural time, indicated by images of planting, and the rejection of that time which sees "the future in the instant." Significantly, Macbeth regards himself as "time's fool."

Paul, Henry N. "The Imperial Theme in *Macbeth*," *Joseph Quincy Adams Memorial Studies* (Washington: Folger Shakespeare Library, 1948), pp. 253–258.

Paul is useful for presenting a partial translation of Gwynn's *Tres Quasi Sibyllae*, the Oxford playlet that honored King James and that bears a close resemblance to the show of kings in IV.i. His article insists that originally this scene of *Macbeth* was a true apotheosis of the Stuart line, not the perfunctory scene that it may be nowadays in acting. He points out that the show of kings because of its Stuart and hence disloyal associations was omitted in Garrick's eighteenth-century version.

Paul, Henry N. *The Royal Play of Macbeth* (New York: Macmillan, 1950).

This important work states the view that *Macbeth* was expressly written for performance before King James and interprets the play as a caressing and cosseting of the monarch's beliefs on witchcraft, genealogy, the permanence of the House of Stuart, and much else. Paul holds that the play was first performed before James I and his brother-in-law, King Christian of Denmark, at Hampton Court on August 7, 1606.

Pyle, Fitzroy. "The Way to Dusty Death," *Notes and Queries*, N. S. 19 (1972), 129–131.

Pyle points out that the speech beginning "To-morrow, and to-morrow, and to-morrow" in V.v has not been analyzed with regard to the internal coherence of its images. Macbeth speaks with the idea in mind of a burial vault. He speaks of life as a procession, of days as mourners, each bearing a candle "to the last syllable of recorded time." They light the way for fools to be buried with the dust of death's decay. The candles make shadows on the wall, and so Macbeth in the coda of the speech turns to the theatre as another species of futility.

Rauber, D. F. "Macbeth, Macbeth, Macbeth," *Criticism*, 11 (1969), 59–67.

Rauber points to three's existing everywhere in *Macbeth*. Structurally three's are seen in Macbeth's rise, his reign, and his fall; in the heaven of an idealized England under "most pious" Edward, in the bleeding earth of Scotland, and in the Hell of the Weird Sisters and Hecate. Relationally, Rauber points to the three victims of Macbeth. The magical aspects of three's are obvious. There are three stages in Macbeth's life with respect to fertility and sterility. Rauber retreats from speculating on what all this means.

Ribner, Irving. *Patterns in Shakespearian Tragedy* (London: Methuen, 1966), pp. 153–167.

This is a solid though not particularly original account of the play.

Rissanen, Matti. "'Nature's Copy,' 'Great Bond,' and 'Lease of Nature' in *Macbeth*," *Neuphilologische Mittelungen*, 70 (1969), 714–723.

This article is an examination of "the lease of life" pattern of imagery seen in the phrases "nature's copy" (*Macbeth*, III.ii.36), "great bond" (III.ii.49), and "lease of Nature (IV.i.99). The basic idea is that man has a contract or "bond" with nature to the effect that man holds his life as his "property" until the moment of his death.

Robertson, Jean, "Macbeth on Sleep: 'Sore Labour's Bath' and

Sidney's 'Astrophil and Stella', XXXIX," *Notes and Queries*, N. S. 14 (1967), 139–141.

This note is useful for presenting classical and Elizabethan analogues to Macbeth's passage on sleep in II.iii.33 ff.

Rogers, H. L. "An English Tailor and Father Garnet's Straw," *Review of English Studies*, 16 (1965), 44–49.

Rogers points out the topicality of the "farmer" and the "tailor" in the Porter's soliloquy, connecting the first with one of Father Garnet's aliases and the second with Hugh Griffin, a tailor, who was examined in late 1606 for complicity in promoting the idea of a miraculous head of straw bearing Garnet's image, supposedly derived from the Jesuit's blood.

Rosen, William. *Shakespeare and the Craft of Tragedy* (Cambridge, Mass.: Harvard Univ. Press, 1960).

In the chapter of *Macbeth* Rosen undertakes to establish the point of view that the audience is expected to take toward Macbeth. He does not favor the pattern-analysis critics who maintain that the audience is not intended to sympathize with the bloody, usurping tyrant. Rosen offers a number of insights derived from common sense that make his chapter worth perusal. For example, he observes that Shakespeare does not present the murder of Duncan onstage, action that would alienate sympathy from Macbeth. He suggests that Macbeth's mental torments universalize the significance of his personal life.

Schanzer, Ernest. "Four Notes on *Macbeth*," *Modern Language Review*, 52 (1957), 223–224.

Schanzer is cogent in explanation and paraphrase of (among other things) *Macbeth*, I.vii.64–67 and III.iv.121–125.

Setterberg, Ruth Elizabeth, *Ceremony and Ceremonials in Macbeth*, unpublished Ph. D. dissertation, Boston University, 1962. Order No. 62-5533.

This dissertation discusses the nature and functions of ceremonial metaphor in *Macbeth*. Setterberg suggests that ceremony and ceremonials contribute to the thematic development of kingship, transgression, and grace; they reinforce the distinction between good and evil; they help to render disorder in nature, man, and society abominable; they direct thought, by such expressions as "poison'd chalice," "Lord's anointed temple," and "trumpet-tongued," to both temporal and eternal matters. The formal salutation of an unworthy sovereign is an ironic effect.

Shakespeare, William. *Macbeth, A New Variorum Edition*, ed. H. H. Furness (Philadelphia: J. B. Lippincott, 1903).
An indispensable repository of eighteenth- and nineteenth-century criticism, arranged for the most part scene-by-scene and line-by-line.

Shakespeare, William. *Macbeth*, ed. Kenneth Muir. The Arden Shakespeare. (1951; rpt. London: Methuen, 1959).
Muir's edition is recommended.

Siegel, Paul N. "Echoes of the Bible Story in *Macbeth*," *Notes and Queries*, N. S. 2 (1955), 142–143.
Siegel exhibits parallels between the story of Macbeth and the histories of Adam, Judas, and Lucifer.

Smith, Grover. "The Naked New-Born Babe in *Macbeth*: Some Iconographical Evidence," *Renaissance Papers*, 1964, pp. 21–27.
This paper presents an iconographic background for *Macbeth*, I.vii.21–23. Smith cites Renaissance maps, paintings, and sculpture.

Spargo, J. W. "The Knocking at the Gate in *Macbeth*," *Joseph Quincy Adams Memorial Studies* (Washington: Folger Shakespeare Library, 1948), pp. 269–277.
Spargo suggests that the knocking on the gate, far from being comic relief, reminded learned Elizabethans of Horace's "Pallida mors aequo pede pulsat..." (pale death kicks with impartial foot the doors of rich and poor) and Elizabethans generally of the rough knocking (with spade handles) of those citizens entrusted with finding and burying those dead of the plague.

Spurgeon, Caroline F. E. *Shakespeare's Imagery and What It Tells Us* (New York: Macmillan, 1936).
Spurgeon, regarding fear as an image, points out that there is no play of Shakespeare's in which this word is more frequently

mentioned, and that it is one of two plays by Shakespeare in which "love" is least used. "The imagery in *Macbeth*," she states, "appears to me to be more rich and varied, more highly imaginative, more unapproachable by any other writer, than that of any other single play." She calls attention to the clothes imagery as suggesting how badly King Macbeth wears his new honors. Another major image is that of reverberating sounds over vast areas. Another is the imagery of light and darkness for good and evil. Yet another in the play is disease for sin. Like Bradley, she notes the ever-recurring images of blood; and she points to the numerous images of animals, usually predatory.

Stallybrass, Peter. "*Macbeth* and Witchcraft," *Focus on Macbeth*, ed. John R. Brown (London: Routledge & Kegan Paul, 1982), pp. 189–209.

Stallybrass argues that witchcraft in *Macbeth* tends to legitimize patriarchy. The play "mobilizes the patriarchal fear of unsubordinated woman, the unstable element to which Krämer and Sprenger [authors of the influential *Malleus Maleficarum*, 1486] attributed the overthrow of 'nearly all the kingdoms of the world' . . . ."

Stewart, J. I. M. *Character and Motive in Shakespeare* (London: Longmans, Green, 1949, rtd. 1950).

In the chapter "Steep Tragic Contrast" Stewart writes to correct E. E. Stoll's view that regards *Macbeth* as being made psychologically incoherent in order to promote aesthetic and dramatic quality. Stewart says: "I conclude, then, that before *Macbeth* we ought not to abandon the conception of a 'psychology' . . . but deepen it." Stewart emphasizes Macbeth's imagination "with its extreme sensibility to sinister and morbid impressions," Macbeth's self-regarding histrionic talent, Shakespeare's obvious thrusting of the action into a primitive past, the pervasiveness of the "ensanguined mist" in the play, and the precipitation with which Shakespeare brings on an early crisis.

Stirling, Brents. *Unity in Shakespearian Tragedy* (New York: Columbia Univ. Press, 1956).

In Chapter 9, "Look, how our partner's rapt," Stirling states: "*Macbeth* is based upon the familiar tragic motive of sin and self-destruction which are compulsive." He discusses four themes that contribute to the "exceptional unity" of the play—darkness, sleep, raptness, and contradiction.

Stoll, E. E. "The Objectivity of the Ghosts in Shakespeare," *Publications of the Modern Language Association*, 22 (1907), 205 ff.

Stoll presents seven cogent reasons arguing the objectivity of Banquo's Ghost in the banquet scene.

Swaminathan, S. R. "The Image of Pity in 'Macbeth,'" *Notes and Queries*, N. S. 17 (1970), 132.

The author suggests that the iconographic representation of the newly escaped soul of a dead man as a small naked child is relevant to a full understanding of *Macbeth*, I.vii.21–23.

Thumboo, Edwin. "Macbeth and the Generous Duncan," *Shakespeare Quarterly*, 22 (1971), 181–186.

Thumboo suggests that Ross's speech in I.iii.89–100, the word "Hail" in I.iii.106 and elsewhere, and Duncan's speech to Macbeth in I.iv.14–21 inflate Macbeth's self-importance to the point where he does not feudally subordinate himself to the King and contribute to his ambitions.

Tromly, Frederic B. "Macbeth and His Porter," *Shakespeare Quarterly*, 26 (1975), 151–156.

Tromly, as against Harcourt, thinks of the Porter not as a contrast to but as a figure for Macbeth. Accordingly he finds analogies between Macbeth and the Porter in virtually every detail of the scene. The effect of all this is to bring Macbeth from the "monstrous" and the "fiendish" toward the "ordinary" and the "human."

Van Doren, Mark. *Shakespeare* (New York: Holt, 1939).

In the chapter on *Macbeth* Van Doren, after discriminating differences in the characterization of Macbeth and his lady, concentrates upon what he regards as major symbols—fear, blood, sleeplessness, and time.

Veszy-Wagner, L. "'Macbeth: 'Fair is Foul and Foul is Fair,'" *American Imago*, 25 (1968), 242–257.

Veszy-Wagner in this article attempts to correct Freud's alleged misunderstanding of *Macbeth* as centering on the theme of childlessness. He views Macbeth's problem as "uncertain identity." Macbeth is torn between loyalty to the king and disloyalty, virility and effeminacy. His disunited parts clash and cause his undoing. Lady Macbeth, a phallic woman, represents both Macbeth himself and the other Lady Macbeth, his mother. Their childlessness is regarded as punishment for Macbeth's indulgence of chaotic infantile murder-fantasies. The Weird Sisters are here viewed as the Satanic counterparts of the Magi, who in the end compass the death of the infanticidal king.

Waithe, Eugene M. "Manhood and Valor in Two Shakespearian Tragedies," *English Literary History*, 17 (1950).
This important article points to two conceptions of manhood in *Macbeth*—the narrower view which regards man solely in terms of physical valor; the larger (and approved) view that includes this but also includes moral awareness. Macduff perhaps best embodies in the play the larger conception of manhood.

Wickham, Glynne, "Hell-Castle and Its Doorkeeper," *Shakespeare Survey 19* (Cambridge: Cambridge Univ. Press, 1966), pp. 68–74.
This article suggests that II.iii is an overlay of the Harrowing of Hell scenes in the English Miracle Cycles. Wickham points out that Hell was in these plays represented as a castle, dungeon, and cesspit. The York and Towneley scribes employed a doorkeeper named Rybald (*O.E.D.* "Scurrilous, irreverent, profane, indecent"). Wickham finds significant the Porter's first question—"Who's there, i' th' name of Belzebub?" Macduff's knocking is suggestive of Christ's knocking on the door of Hell to release the souls of the patriarchs and prophets from Satan. Generally, the Porter is Rybald and dreams he is in Hell. Wickham thinks the scene suggestive, once it is recognized as an overlay, of what to expect from Macduff, who has not yet been identified as avenger of Duncan's murder.

Williams, George Walton. "The Third Murderer in *Macbeth*," *Shakespeare Quarterly*, 23 (1972), 261.
Williams corroborates the view that the Third Murderer cannot

be Macbeth because of Shakespeare's undeviating adherence at this time in his life to the "Law of Re-entry," *i.e.*, one character who walks offstage at the end of a scene does not walk onstage before the first line of the following scene.

Wood, James O. "'Fillet of a Fenny Snake,'" *Notes and Queries*, N. S. 12 (1965), 332–233.

Wood argues that "fillet" in "Fillet of a fenny snake" (IV.i.12) means not "slice," the usual gloss, but "the ribbon of its cast scarf-skin." The source is Golding's translation of Ovid.

Wood, James O. "Hecate's 'Vaprous Drop, Profound," *Notes and Queries*, N. S. (1964), 262–264.

Wood suggests that "profound," III.v.24, is from Latin *profundere,* "to pour forth" rather than from Latin *profundus*, "deep."

Wood, James O. "Lady Macbeth's Suckling," *Notes and Queries*, N. S. 11 (1964), 137–138.

Wood suggests Ovid's account of Athamas as the source of *Macbeth*, I.vii.54–59, thus exculpating Shakespeare for conceiving the horrid thought of a parent's dashing out an infant's brains.

Wren, Robert M. "The Hideous Trumpet and Sexual Transformation in *Macbeth*," *Forum*, 4 (1967), 18–21.

This article suggests without overt reference to Renaissance hierarchical thinking that Macbeth, in yielding to his wife in the murder of Duncan, has surrendered his masculine-rational power and has become all appetite.

Zitner, Sheldon P. "*Macbeth* and the Moral Scale of Tragedy," *Journal of General Education*, 16 (1964-65), 20–28.

A reading of this article is valuable for suggesting those matters in *Macbeth* that prevent its being regarded as melodrama: among other things, the narration of some events, use of agents at times instead of the protagonist, delicate evocation of the power of witchcraft, suggestions of Macbeth's passional relationship to his wife, the Porter's generalizing of human evil, Malcolm's intimations of suspicion toward men in general in the testing of Macduff, and Banquo's statement of human beings as giving way in repose to evil.